P

T

INCUBATED
AUTHOR

FINALLY: A tangible slice of inspiration for those of us that are building businesses based on helping other people improve their lives. As Angela Lauria says, "The right book can ignite an adventure that draws your people to you", and now in her new Start a Movement program and book, she actually teaches the logistics of how to get your book into the hands of your people & what to do with them once they come. In a self help world that can often involve circular conversations and dreams that don't translate into actually being able to financially support yourself so that you can help your people, this book and movement is like nothing else. Start a Movement is about taking action and truly making sh!t happen...not just talkin' about it.

RANDI RUBENSTEIN

Reading this book will help aspiring (and previously unsuccessful) authors understand why they've been running around chasing their tails! The combination of inspiration and get 'er done wisdom make it a great guide for anyone who's stuck trying to figure out what to write, why to write, and how to make a living from your movement. I highly recommend it for people who know they're here to help the world...but find themselves stuck at the starting gate.

NANCY MARMOLEJO

The Incubated Author is a must-read for anyone who wants more than just to have written a book. This is for someone who is ready to effect change in the world. I read The Difference (also by Angela Lauria), and used her innovative process to write two extremely successful books. The Incubated Author is the next—and most important, IMHO—step of the journey. Life-changing books don't happen by accident—they are carefully crafted to ensure that the message is clear, and that the call to action is unavoidable. Ms. Lauria has helped dozens of authors do exactly that, and now she's sharing the process with the world. You won't just write a book following this process—you'll start a revolution.

JILL ANGIE

Angela Lauria's new book, "The Incubated Author", is a marvelously entertaining mixture of solid PR/marketing wisdom and what some would call airy-fairy, woo-woo stuff. For me, it was exactly those energy-related and spiritually focused elements of the book which made me love it. Not that I didn't eat up the experience and expertise Dr Lauria shared—she clearly knows her topic. It was the combination of the two, a combination I have not seen done so well as this book does, that made reading it, then rereading parts of it, then going back to make sure I grokked it, which hooked me. Highly recommended for any would-be author with a movement in their heart which needs to be started!

RICK HAMRICK

Beautifully written. The Incubated Author is straightforward, honest, motivating and inspiring.

A. REYBURN

Angela Lauria's "The Incubated Author—10 steps to start a movement with your message" delighted me with its authentic & practical message, expressed with passion, sparkle and lots of experience. Lauria powerfully articulates the importance of clarity and commitment in starting a movement with one's message, and goes the distance in describing each step of the journey (often a "hero's journey") in seven well-researched, well-written chapters. This is a terrific book—practical, philosophical and comprehensive—for those who want to make a difference in the world by sharing their transformative message.

MARY MARTIN

Wisdom just flows through the pages of this book. If you're called to write a book, read this one! Thank you, Angela Lauria, for sharing your messages so powerfully and clearly—again.

ESTHER GOLDENBERG

The Incubated Author turns how you think about writing a book on its head. It forces you to get crystal clear about who the book is for, how they will be different and how to create a movement with your message— BEFORE you ever start writing. When you get that clarity up front, you write a book that can beautifully support your vision, attract the people that most need your message and grow your business. Angela Lauria is a master at this and she's doing what no one else in publishing is doing today.

SHARON POPE
Love Coach

Want to know how to step away from your own ego and insecurities so that you can finally make the difference in the world that you are called to make? This is your book! Angela pulls it all together—how to write the right book, fund your movement, but also how to think, hold yourself accountable and step into being the leader that you are called to be, while you keep your soul and the integrity of your message intact!

MAGGIE HUFFMAN

Angela writes in such a direct and inspiring way that I can't wiggle my way out of what it is I need to do. She puts the mantle on those who are being prompted to share their truths with the world. I recommend taking advantage of her wisdom.

JERRE ADER M.S.
LPC LifeCoach

The Incubated Author changed my life. Angela has written about what, up until now, had been the missing link for me. I'm here to start a movement, and any inertia or distraction I've experienced up until now stems from the fact that I had not yet stepped into that truth. This book has lit a fire in me, and I have never felt more ready to step up and be seen in the world. This shift has given me so much energy! I now understand that when you're walking your path in complete integrity, your life force increases to allow you to step up to the challenge.

In "The Incubated Author," Angela describes her strategic approach to crafting your book, and it is pure genius.

If you're starting a movement with your message, and if you're looking for everything to come into crystal clear focus, read this book. You'll be so glad you did. I know I am. Thank you, Angela, for sharing your unique insights and giving me the excitement and energy to really go for it.

BRIGID DINEEN

Brilliant! Angela Lauria beautifully lays out exactly how to not just write a book, but create a movement with it. If you want to be an author who inspires action, passion and has the power to create a community, you need to read The Incubated Author before you write another word. Lauria gently steers the reader away from the common pitfalls of writing a book that reaches no one. Then she gives the blueprint of exactly how to write a book that sparks energy in it's readers. If you're writing a self-help book, do yourself a favor and read this one first.

ANDREA HANSON

THE INCUBATED AUTHOR

10 STEPS TO START A MOVEMENT WITH YOUR MESSAGE

BY ANGELA E. LAURIA

Cover Design: John Matthews

Interior Design: Heidi Miller

Editing: Mila Nedeljkov & Maggie McReynolds

Author's photo courtesy of John Matthews

DEDICATION

Before I had a message...

Before I wanted a movement...

There was a reason.

That reason, my reason for playing big even when
it's so damn uncomfortable, is my son **Jesse**.

I hope someday this book and the results
will make him proud to be its inspiration.

TABLE OF CONTENTS

The Next Three Steps to Starting
Your Movement

STEP TWO:
Notice Likely Apostles

STEP THREE:
Communicate Shared Suffering

STEP FOUR:
Understand Your Enemy

Inside the Author Incubator
On Market Validation

39

CHAPTER TWO
THE TRUTH ABOUT
MAKING A DIFFERENCE

STEP FIVE:
Baptize the New Bliss

5 5

CHAPTER THREE
CREATING THE RIGHT BOOK TO IGNITE YOUR MOVEMENT

CHAPTER FOUR

Architecting Your Mission

Define Your Ideal Reader

Identify Your Voice

Frame Your Outcome

Focus Your Author Mojo

Envision Your Success

Release Your Blocks

Establish Your Author Feeling State

Nurture Your Manuscript

Create Your Masterpiece

Expand Your Reach

Inside the Author Incubator
On Who to Write For

CHAPTER SEVEN
CLEAR EYES, FULL HEARTS, CAN'T LOSE

ABOUT DIFFERENCE PRESS

Let's Start a Movement with
Your Message

"Yes, I'm ready!"

OTHER BOOKS BY
DIFFERENCE PRESS

THE INCUBATED AUTHOR—AN INTRODUCTION

"YOUR WORK IS TO DISCOVER YOUR WORLD AND THEN WITH ALL YOUR HEART GIVE YOURSELF TO IT."

BUDDHA

There was a lot of nervous laughter and shuffling when I asked them to write the list of reasons they should NOT be allowed to lead a movement. I gave them 10 minutes to write freely, and not one pen came up off the page. Not a second of writer's block in the house. The reasons kept flowing.

"I don't even know what my movement is."

"I'm overweight and not attractive enough for TV."

"I may not actually be smart enough."

"I haven't sold anything yet."

"I'm still not healed all the way."

"I don't even really want people to know what I'm doing."

"Actually, honestly, I'm not that good of a writer."

"I don't have the right qualifications."

"Someone else already has a book or movement on this topic."

"I don't have the organizational skills to run a movement."

"I wouldn't have anything particularly relevant to share."

The timer buzzed, the nervous giggles continued, and there was almost a sense of relief in the room.

"Look through your list," I said, "and be sure that if I ask you, you could give me three pieces of evidence supporting that each of your statements is true." I quizzed a couple of them to be sure they knew how serious I was. I didn't cross-examine their evidence.

I gave my next assignment.

"Now, re-write those sentences flipping all the negative statements to positive ones." They squirmed and struggled. Instead of the 10 minutes it took to originally write them, reversing the sentences took at least twice as long. It wasn't hard—their brains were just frozen by the weight of the request.

I asked them to share again.

"I'm flexible and can easily adapt as my movement takes shape."

"I am the perfect weight for the followers I want."

"My healing journey will be important to my followers."

"I'm a good-enough writer."

"I do have the right qualifications."

"No one else can write the same book as me."

"I would have anything particularly relevant to share."

"Now," I said calmly. "Give me three reasons why the opposite is also true."

I scanned the room. Meka gave me some of her reasons first, then Sasha, followed by Jodi. Each provided evidence that the OPPOSITE of their biggest fear was true. They were convincing reasons, too.

And that's when I broke the news to them. There is no such thing as truth about a matter like this. You are only, ever, exactly as qualified to lead a movement as YOU decide you are.

Or not.

STEP ONE:
INSPIRE BY ANOINTING YOURSELF

Could we find evidence you aren't cut out for this? Sure can, all day long. Could we find evidence your followers couldn't be luckier to have you? Yup, that too. There is no way to prove either statement to be true, so let's pick the one that feels better to us.

Who decides whether you are good enough or worthy enough to start a movement? There is just no possible answer to this question except you. If anyone else tried to decide, let's say me, for example, what would be the authority on which I stand? Nothing testable for sure.

What about Spirit, Source, or God? Could that be the arbiter? Sure! I'm all in for that! But who would have access to that information and what would it look like? Your relationship with Source, if you have one, is yours and yours alone. I would posit, however, that if the idea of starting a movement is coming up for you, that's exactly the Universe's way of letting you know what it has in mind for you.

You and you alone can decide if you should start a movement.

And this is the good news. Your authority and worthiness can never be threatened, because you hold the keys to them. And because only you can decide if you should start a movement, this decision is among the boldest acts of courage and one of your first gifts to your movement. When you anoint yourself as the leader of this movement, you inspire your followers. In fact, *until* you accept your role as leader in your heart, until you anoint yourself, you won't have followers at all. And it's your followers who transform you from a person with a message to the leader of a movement.

Self-anointing has a long and ancient history. When you anoint yourself, you are given a new heart along with the ability to control our emotions in new ways, new words, new abilities to share our message, new followers, and new means to surround them and support them. It is also said that we are given new enemies, because great leaders have great enemies, and new authority, so that we may be trusted to show humility, honor, and confidence in decision-making.

I know you think this is about your movement and the people you are here to help, and there is no doubt that it is. But even more than that, it's about you in a leadership role. It's about the identity you need to embody to make this movement work.

Martin Luther King, Jr. once said, "Whatever affects one directly, affects all indirectly. I can never be what I ought to be until you are what you ought to be. This is the interrelated structure of reality." At the core, it's that structure of reality that we'll be exploring in this book.

In Chapter One, we'll determine who your movement is serving, we'll identify their shared suffering, we'll come to understand your enemies, and we will be able to notice your likely early followers. In Chapter Two, we'll align the beliefs and values of your followers, and identify what bright outcome we are moving toward and which details we are hoping to fix. In Chapter Three, we dig into your Hero's Journey, draw together your influences, and then BAM! It's time to create a book that makes a difference. In Chapter Four, I show you exactly how to create and launch a book that ignites a call to adventure for your mission. Chapter Five is all about what "Funding Your Mission" takes. You'll learn the mechanisms and milestones to measure your success, how to create a tipping point, and how to create the easiest, simplest model to really fund your movement. And in Chapter Six, you'll see what it's going to take, and understand my wish for you at the end of this, when you can see what the next five or so years would look like if you're really committed to your movement. My goal is that by the end of this book you can, with clarity and intention, go all in and face some of the challenges of leading a movement with "clear eyes and full hearts."

CHAPTER ONE

WHY START A MOVEMENT?

WHERESOEVER YOU GO, GO WITH
ALL YOUR HEART.

KONGZI

This book is about more than writing a book. *The Incubated Author* has a bigger vision. A vision for each book to become a piece of the puzzle, a step to starting a movement that matters, to having a following of hundreds, thousands, and, someday, millions. Starting a Movement is about understanding all the steps that I've discovered from working with authors over the last five years who wanted more than a book. My entire career has been spent with authors who wanted to write books and sell lots of copies, but in the last five years I've really focused on working with authors who want to start a movement with their message.

What are the things that make a movement? How can you take a book that can make a difference for one person and turn that into a movement with hundreds or thousands or millions of followers? How do you build a tribe? How do you nurture that tribe? How do you show people a new way of thinking about a problem?

If you're familiar with my work, you know that I have a very particular meaning in mind when I talk about making a difference. Making a difference is about having a powerful message of hope, healing, transformation, change, and revolution, but it's also about getting that message into peoples' hearts and hands and actually making tangible, measurable differences in their life.

You aren't making a difference if somebody doesn't know about your idea, even if it's the best idea in the world.

What I have seen with my authors who really break through and start a movement is that, yes, they have that concrete transformative message, but they're also doing the work that it takes to get that message to people.

If you think about the message that Jesus had—and it doesn't matter what your feelings are about Jesus—but he had a message, and let's say that he sat down in his living room and took a nap instead of sharing it. That message, it could have been the best message in the world, but in order to spread the word, he had to go get disciples, and he had to get apostles, and he had to get out there in a very vulnerable way. This is not a pleasant experience all the time.

A SERVANT'S HEART

To make a difference, I truly believe you have to be willing to be uncomfortable, to be willing to share your message with people, and to really put yourself out there. Not on behalf of your ego, because I really don't think that works, and even if it did, I wouldn't be super-interested in it. But on behalf of the people whose lives you want revolutionize.

I talk about having a servant's heart, and often my clients have such a pretty image of what having a servant's heart would be. I think they picture Mother Theresa washing the feet of the lepers, and they're thinking, "Yes, I'm a servant, I would love to do that." But so often, having a servant's heart looks a lot different than that, and really being in a place to serve has a lot to do with building your own leadership muscle, building your own boundary muscle, and becoming an object in motion. Becoming a forward-moving being. Inertia works powerfully in all of our lives, and so, there is a strong desire to not move forward and not take action until we know if it's perfect or we know if it's going to work, or if we know that it's valuable–we want empirical data that it will be valuable. But those things don't come first. It works the opposite.

I was overweight for a very long time, and I thought, when I lose weight, then I will feel good, wear pretty clothes, and love taking pictures of myself. What I learned was, I had to feel those things and do those things in order to lose weight. And it's the same thing about building a movement with your message. You will need to be the leader of that movement before there are even followers, and, as their number grows, your leadership will always need to be one step ahead of them.

Recently, I was talking to a client. She is a ship's captain, she has a sailboat in the Caribbean, and she was saying that one of the most important things she's learned about being on her boat is that if you are not in motion—if you are just docked in the harbor—you can't steer the ship. There's no steering functionality. You could stand at the helm and you can move the ship's wheel but you won't go in any particular direction.

So many of the authors who have told me they want to make a difference and they want to have a tribe of followers are standing parked in the harbor, with the anchor down and the lines tied, and I watch them steering the steering wheel, but not really going anywhere.

In this book we are going to explore how you get the ship in motion. How you become the leader of your movement—even before the movement is where you think it needs to be—to be that leader.

One of the keys to doing that is making your success and the success of your movement inevitable.

What are the actions that you need to take to make your movement inevitable?

One of the ways that I look at that, is to look at the people who have built a movement. What did they do? And what can we learn from them? What did they do intentionally, maybe, but subconsciously as well. Will a book be a part of it? Sure! You know I love books, but we need to understand what your movement even is before we can write a book that's going to beautifully feed into that movement.

A lot of people will come to me and they'll say, "I really want to start a revolution in self-care." Or they'll say, "I want to start a revolution among young women because I want them to all know they're good enough." Or they'll say, "I want to start a movement for graphic designers and other freelancers, so they're charging what they want to charge." But they haven't really thought through what that movement looks like. Are we rallying? Are we all going to get on bicycles in Portland? How will you know you have a movement? And in order to write a book that is going to support that movement in the best possible way, we have to know what that movement's going to look like, and then we have to get people in a position where they are begging to be a part of it, when they're so clear on where they're going they can't wait to jump on board.

A book will be a part of that, but it has to be the right book.

THE SELLING LOTS OF BOOKS FALLACY

The first thing you need to know is that most book marketing information in the marketplace today is about selling books. Most book marketing techniques are designed to drive book sales. While it may seem counter-intuitive, focusing on how to sell the most books is *not* the most productive way to create your book or to support your movement. A book that would sell lots of copies has different qualities than a book that makes a difference and a book that starts a movement. That doesn't mean you won't sell book copies, but you need to understand a little bit about the traditional publishing industry and the liminal phase in which we find ourselves in the world of publishing.

Traditional publishers operate like a casino, and they will place bets on ten or twenty or thirty or a hundred different authors, knowing that only a fraction of those are going to be successful. What they are doing is covering their bets. They're placing bets across the spectrum, knowing every book isn't going to hit, but the goal for each of the books is book sales. So, when you work with a traditional publisher, you get an editor and you get a designer, and the editor and the designer and the other book publishing professionals that you work with, they are working for the publisher, they are working on behalf of the publisher's interest.

The publisher has purchased the rights to your intellectual property, and their job is to "exploit" those rights. That's what the advance bought them, and now they're trying to make the most of their bet, and the way that they're going to do that is by optimizing your book for book sales. That may mean, when you look at the book cover, that it makes no sense to you, but it's something they think is going to connect with a hot market and make you more of a more likely *American Idol winner* rather than the stand-out contestant.

Really weird or really controversial or really stand-out ideas are not good bets. Jesus would have been a terrible bet for a publisher today. They would have been much more interested in a book by the Roman Emperor of the day, because it would be a guaranteed bestseller.

If you are trying to start a movement with your book, you are not going to be in a position to have the most book sales, which is great news, because we don't want the most book sales. We want the most rabid people to buy your book. In other words, we don't have a target of two billion Christians, what we're looking for right now are those first twelve Jews to get behind the idea of you being the Messiah. We are looking for those most dedicated, most bought-in people, people who are really ready to be a part of your movement—to be your apostles.

Your first twelve apostles are the people that are in the most pain and the most prepared to get out of that pain, to see the light and to join your cause, whatever that cause is.

What I see happen with people who have the dream of starting a movement with their message is that they spend tons of time trying to get that message right, but they're trying to get it right the wrong way. They're either asking themselves questions or they're directly asking other people.

What is so much better than asking people if they like the wording, or the logo, or your new website, or whatever it is you're doing, is to actually take the risk of putting it out there and see if people respond in the real world. Go have a sales conversation, or set up a sales page and drive traffic and see if they buy. So, rather than asking people, "Hey, would you buy this?," do some real-life experimenting. This is called market validation.

Before you even write your book, before you get really committed, in your head, to the wording of your movement, let's see if we can "sell" it. How do you know you have the makings of a movement?

Get followers on a Facebook page

Get clicks on a Google Adwords ad

Get sign-ups for a free call

Post a flyer in your local coffee shop and get calls to a phone number

Don't worry about whether you can fulfill the expectations of the callers. You can put them on a waiting list and tell them it's coming. You just want to see if you can make the phone ring or your inbox fill up.

THE 'OOPS I WROTE THE WRONG BOOK' MISTAKE

One of the biggest mistakes I see people make is that they write the wrong book. They write the wrong book because while they're incredibly focused on getting the message out there, they don't even know if they believe it. They're not even all bought in.

I have seen the power of our programs, the power of our ability to launch a book into the world, and the almost negative power that comes up if you write the wrong book. When you have a book, you move your career forward light years faster than people without a book. You might be two or three or even four years down the line in your business by adding book, but if you don't write the right book, we're pushing you four years down the line in the wrong direction.

Having that market validation, is a concept I've adapted from Eric Ries' book, *The Lean Startup.* He calls that product you test with a Minimum Viable Product, or MVP. What's the smallest notion of a movement that you can get people enrolled into?

Author Janette Dalgliesh wrote a two-part series with us. Her books, *Your Everyday Superpower* and *Mastering Your Everyday Superpower,* are two of the best we've ever published, and they are written for skeptics of the law of attraction, to help them see the link between LOA and hardcore brain science. Janette is a beautiful writer, and at the time that she wrote the book she was really excited about working with skeptics of the law of attraction. Until she worked with skeptics of the law of attraction.

It turns out that if you love the law of attraction, it's no fun to spend your time with people who doubt that the law of attraction really works. Janette definitely had a book that could start a movement. She had a ton of interests, clients, and the market validation we'd be looking for, but what she didn't have is the passion to be the leader of that movement. Today Janette calls herself a Soul Archaeologist, Brain Whisperer, and Joy Pilot, and is running a website called Identity Shift Ninja. She's totally passionate about her mission to wreak more joy in the world using brain science and LOA, but her new positioning does not attract very many skeptics, which is just more fun to her. That's not to say you can't be the leader of a movement of skeptics, but now Janette doesn't have to explain brain science four times a day, and her clients have something solid to give their doubting loved ones. But her books weren't the right ones to start the movement she's passionate about.

To start a movement the right way, you want to make sure you're writing the right book, and we do this with market validation. You can test your ideas with ads, Facebook posts, blog posts, guest articles, and in other ways where we can see if people actually take action rather than just telling us they will.

Eric Reis says this approach "isn't simply about spending less money. Lean isn't just about failing fast, failing cheap. It is about putting a process, a methodology around the development of a product." For our purposes, it's taking this from his ideas of product development to movement development—but the principals test out.

If people are not feeling your message, if they won't sign up for a free call or an eBook preorder, for instance, we either need to change the message or we need to change the communications around the message. Of course, the other obvious mistake that people who want to start a movement make is that they don't write a book at all, and if you want to have a movement the number one most critical component is having a book. There are lots of reasons for that, starting with the credibility it gives you as the author of that book, and the media opportunities and the speaking opportunities that come with being an author, but also, and perhaps most importantly, attracting those first 12 apostles. I don't think that your first book about your movement needs to be a $50,000 or 5-million copy bestseller like a Malcolm Gladwell book in order for us to be able to generate significant evidence that you are starting a movement.

Building that evidence, to me, is so much more important than the book sales, because if the book sales end there, who cares whether you sold the book if you haven't been able to rally people to be a part of your cause, if you haven't really changed people, if you haven't made the difference that you've committed to making at the beginning of the process. All you have is a book. And by the way, building that evidence also usually means you make money. Sometimes more money that you can selling books.

You with me?

THE LESS IMPORTANT THAN A 'LOST DOG' MISTAKE

The next mistake that I see is that when starting a movement, people focus on being perfect. The truth is, there is no way to get it perfect because there is no arbiter of perfect. I say, if you really care about this movement and the people who this movement is going to help, then start now. Start your movement with flyers. Start your movement with crappy free websites. Why would you do that? Why would you put it out imperfectly? Because you care about the people on the other side of the revolution! If you're really doing it for your people, you'll put up an imperfect website. You'll get your message out there, even if it's homemade flyers posted on a billboard at Panera.

Think about this. What if your mission in life was to get your lost dog back. Yes, some beautifully designed posters may be nice, but time is of the essence. You need to get your dog back, and I want you to have that same urgency with your movement. The idea of waiting to put it out perfectly would almost kill you because you know what that would be doing to your people.

THE OPRAH MISTAKE

I talk to people who want to write a book all the time. One of the first things I ask is, "What would success with your book look like?" Sometimes they tell me it's helping just one person, or just writing it and finishing it. But most of the time, when I peel back the layers, there is a secret desire. A desire to be on *Oprah* or on the TED mainstage. Some people have told me, "I want a million followers on Facebook," or "I want a million-dollar advance from Random House." They're so focused on those specific outcomes that they can't see the next steps in front of them.

Picturing the million-dollar advance or the special segment on the O Network actually BLOCKS you from being able to see the next steps in front of you that are REQUIRED before Oprah or TED or Random House come knocking. Just hoping "I'll just write something really good and then I'm going to be discovered" is like playing the lottery. That might be fine if it was just about vanity or ego, but if we have a revolution to start, if we have peoples' lives to change, we don't have time to hope that we get plucked out of a line or selected randomly in a lottery.

Can you imagine doing that if you lost your dog? Just hoping someone turned up with your pooch with no effort of your own? It kind of sounds crazy when you think about it like that. It's almost like you don't really love your dog that much or don't mind if he's gone forever. Is that how you feel about the people you want to help?

THE NEXT THREE STEPS TO
STARTING YOUR MOVEMENT

The first thing that every movement needs is a vision. Now, you probably think you have that vision, but I want you to work through this process with me, which will include that market validation we talked about so that we can find out if your vision is viable. If your vision isn't connecting and resonating with other people, we may need to change the message, we may need to change the places where that message is heard, or we may need to change the market you are targeting with the message. Until we know who wants this message, where we can find them, and what the message is, we actually don't want you writing the book, because I don't want you to end up with a book that isn't for your people and I don't want you to end up with a book that it isn't right for you.

Writing the wrong book is like posting notices about your lost dog inside libraries in San Francisco when you last saw your dog running through Central Park near where you live in New York City.

STEP TWO:
NOTICE LIKELY APOSTLES

Let's start off with who you want to make a difference to. This is the person you most want to change. This is the step that almost everyone skips, or just assumes, "I'm the target market, so I already know who I'm serving." And really, that's a movement that falls apart. That is definitely not what is going to get your movement to the next level, because people are surprising.

Even though you may have been that person at one point, it takes a lot of work to remember what you were thinking and feeling before things changed for you. I want you to actually define the person you're trying to serve, think of this person as your apostle. Who is your ideal revolutionary? Who is the person that you most want to convert, and who will go out on your behalf and convert more people? Who is your "John the Baptist?"

This is an individual person. It could be a composite for you, but even this composite must be based on people who really exist, who have real problems. The way that they describe their problems may not be—in fact, almost certainly is not—the way you describe your problems.

I want you to think about three people that you're trying to serve. Name them, describe what they look like, what they do for fun, what their frustrations are, and how they would explain their frustrations. What are they looking for?

These first people we're looking for, for you, are the early adopters. They're at the bleeding edge. These particular people are not going to be the mainstream when this is a mainstream idea, these are the people to help you start the movement, and so, there is something special about these early adopters. That's why we're not just going for mass book sales. If we were, I would tell you to write another *Twilight* book or another *Harry Potter* book, but what we're going for is building a movement, so what we need here are apostles and disciples to spread the word.

STEP THREE:
COMMUNICATE SHARED SUFFERING

The next step in making a difference is to identify a shared oppression or shared pain among the people who are likely to be your early adopters, so we need to understand your future disciples' lives now. We need to understand the "before" so that we can create the "after" in a way that will resonate with them.

Let's say you want to have a revolution for freelancers. You think all freelancers should be unionized. The next question to ask is, what is the shared pain of the people who are likely to be the first people to get on board with your movement?

Sara Horowitz, the founder of the Freelancer's Union, is, according to their website, "the daughter of a labor lawyer and granddaughter of a vice president of the International Ladies' Garment Workers' Union." Now, her reason for starting this movement might be about carrying on a family tradition or because she believes in the labor movement. Sara might believe freelancers are being exploited and that in order for freelancers to have a chance, they need the benefits of collective bargaining in order to get affordable insurance.

But you know what? Those early adopter freelancers probably weren't thinking about America's long history of Worker's Rights. They were probably thinking something like, "I need to get paid more and I need to stop having to deal with crazy clients at 3 a.m."

Your job here is to communicate that shared suffering, that shared pain, something you agree with but that your early adopters would also recognize for themselves before they are fully converted. You need to understand what their life is now, "before," and what it's going to be after the revolution has been a success.

Here's something from the Freelancer's Union, right on their homepage:

"8 out of 10 freelancers get stiffed by deadbeat clients. Annually, an unpaid freelancer loses an average of $6000 in income due to client nonpayment."

Whoa Nelly! That sounds painful! $6K in lost income for 80% of freelancers! Now we're talking! Much more powerful than a dissertation on the rise of the 40-hour work week.

What problem are you solving, and do the people you want in your movement want that problem solved?

You want to solve self-care and self-love, and you want to help people through a transition, and you want people to meditate so that they aren't so filled with anxiety, but the part you are not clear on is, what does your ideal apostle want to be seen wanting? What is the problem that they want solved? What's driving them crazy? How is it holding them back? What is the cost to them of staying where they are, and why can't they get there without you?

STEP FOUR:
UNDERSTAND YOUR ENEMY

You know what all powerful movements have? An enemy! You can't be the hero if there isn't a villain. Every movement needs an anti-movement; every revolution has to have a dictator. Your movement isn't necessarily about destroying this bad guy, but we want to put you in contrast to someone or something. It helps us ground ourselves in what the revolution is that you're bringing and what the revolution isn't.

There has to be someone who would be totally against your movement in order for your movement to be something to fight FOR. I'm going to go back to my buddy Jesus, because Jesus' whole message was about love, right? Who can be against that? Everyone's "all in" for love. But Jesus wasn't really about love, he was about loving your enemies. Love even if someone's trying to kill you. He was about love even when somebody was a criminal. He was about love even in the face of being publicly shamed. And many people were really against this, because they felt like it was impractical and unsafe and just a generally terrible idea. There are still people today, clearly, who are against that.

One of our bestselling authors, Jill Angie, has written several books about running for women of all shapes, sizes, and speeds. You might ask, "Who would be against women running?" You know those pickup trucks that go with the "No Fat Chicks" sign in the back window, that sticker? Those people! That's who! Body Shamers are the enemy of Jill's movement. And there is no shortage of Body Shamers who feel perfectly justified in their quest to live in a world of smaller women.

Without an enemy, you can't get followers and you can spread the word with your message. You can make a difference, but a movement needs you to construct a bad guy.

I don't want you to vilify your enemy. I want you to understand your enemy so that you can know who your movement is *not* for. Not because they're bad or shouldn't have a movement, but because your enemy needs to be defined narrowly enough that it's an identifiable group. An individual person, or "all men," or "all of Western society," or "all of anyone who doesn't believe in love"—these are not helpful enemies. We want to have a group that we can identify. They don't have to be currently around, so it can be something from the past. Who would be totally irrelevant if your movement succeeded?

By the way, this is what PR agencies do all the time, and it is a really key part of corporate communications. Even Apple has a bad guy, I bet you know who it is, and Apple's done a really great job of making PC the bad guy. Remember those fantastic Apple vs. PC commercials from a few years back? But has PC made Mac the bad guy? Well, they tried a couple of times, but they don't really have a movement, they have a commodity. See, not having an enemy doesn't mean that no one will ever buy your stuff or you won't make a difference, but what I really want to focus on are the commonalities, whether conscious or not, among people who really have a movement with their message, not just a book that matters.

In the next chapter we're going to talk about actually starting the movement, but in order to make a difference, you need to be very clear on who you're trying to make a difference for, what the shared pain or discomfort that they would all admit to is, and who the bad guy is in your story. Then, we can start to make some magic.

INSIDE THE AUTHOR INCUBATOR
On Market Validation

Q: I'm thinking, it would be really cool to run my ideas for my movement by actual people, rather than act it out ourselves? Is there any reason I shouldn't do that?

A: When you ask people, you're tainting the research, because they will always tell you what they think you want to hear. Even if you said to somebody, "Don't tell me what you think you want me to hear," they will be doing just that because you, as a researcher, are affecting your research.

Surveys and quizzes and asking doesn't work, that's why we're talking about market validation. For instance, try this: Come up with the name of your movement and do a free call by that same name. Let's say you did a free call titled "Free Your Inner Author." If nobody comes to that free call, you haven't found the messaging yet. If they won't pay the price of their email address, then you know.

Now you could call ten of the people who saw the ad for your free call and never clicked on it and you could ask them, "Hey, I'm doing a free call, do you think it's a good idea? Here's the name of it." I guarantee you eight out of ten of them will tell you they love it and they will be there. But when you actually ask them to sign up, they take no action, so that isn't it.

It seems like a good idea. I really wish it was.

This is exactly where most people go wrong, so your urge is normal.

CHAPTER TWO

THE TRUTH ABOUT MAKING A DIFFERENCE

"IF YOUR ACTIONS INSPIRE OTHERS TO
DREAM MORE, LEARN MORE,
DO MORE AND BECOME MORE,
YOU ARE A LEADER."

JOHN QUINCY ADAMS

In Chapter One, we asked who your movement is in service of. What is their shared suffering, and who's the "bad guy," or enemy of your movement? In this chapter, we are going to get serious about what it takes to move these early adopter prospects you've identified to take action and join your movement.

STEP FIVE:

BAPTIZE THE NEW BLISS

Back in 2014, Nancy Duarte presented some research at the World Domination Summit in Portland, Oregon that I found fascinating. She says that to persuade an audience, you need to create a tension between what is and what could be. She calls that possible future, when they adopt your ideas, the "New Bliss." I'm going to borrow that term in this book with credit to her. Duarte says we need to alternate between reminding people of the current status they're in and then revealing the path to a better alternative. By doing this, she explains, we create a conflict that needs to be resolved. Without that gap between what is and what could be, there is a temptation to accept that the way things are is the way they must be.

The next thing we need to know is what you will build to replace the old paradigm. What are we working towards? You need to have a crystal-clear vision of a new reality that we could be living in. The messaging app, Slack, offers a crystal-clear reality of life without email. Kind Bars has a crystal-clear vision of snacks with real ingredients, where you can read the ingredients on the labels and understand what they are. Tom's Shoes has a crystal-clear vision of a buying economy where wealthy shoppers subsidize under-developed commodity needs of the underprivileged, and enjoy doing it.

If we were to paint the biggest picture possible of what this new paradigm is for your movement and we go beyond your early adopters, past the tipping point to the mainstream adoption where just about everyone's involved in your vision, how is that world different?

For Slack, in its New Bliss, email is dead.

For Kind Bars, in its New Bliss, highly processed food is dead.

For Tom's Shoes, in its New Bliss, basic commodities like water and shoes are available to all at prices they can afford.

What's the new world that your ideal reader is going to live in? Now, this doesn't mean we're going to be there tomorrow, right? We're going to get grounded in reality, but I want you to see the power of having this vision in your head.

Martin Luther King, Jr. had this vision. He said, "I have a dream that, one day, this nation will rise up and live out the true meaning of its creed that all men were created equal." His image is that this *nation*, not just black people or oppressed people, will rise up—that's the New Bliss (not the later-this-week bliss but the somewhat-distant-future bliss that he held space for on our behalf). He continued, "I have a dream that, one day, my four little children will live in a nation where they'll not be judged by the color of their skin but by the content of their character. I have a dream that, one day, little black boys and little black girls will be able to join hands with little white boys and little white girls as sisters and brothers."

We live that New Bliss now, right? And, obviously, I'm not saying there aren't still racial issues, but that specific dream that he characterized, we've seen that dream play out for many of us in our lifetimes.

I want you to write your own "I Have a Dream" speech and to really get clear on what the world would look

like if your movement actually succeed
"happily ever after" when we're done
ment, when it's worked, what could the
I want you to have these concrete images so that p
know what they're working towards, and so that they
trust you to hold space for that bigger vision. Even if
you weren't around to run your movement anymore,
people will know, this is the vision we're marching to.
In fact, Live Your Legend founder Scott Dinsmore
isn't around to run his movement anymore. He died
tragically in a 2015 mountain climbing accident, but
his movement continues on.

When MLK gave his very first speech, he didn't have
the exact, same audience that he had for the "I Have a
Dream" speech on the steps of the Lincoln Memorial.
It was a different audience. So, tomorrow, you're not
going to have the Lincoln Memorial-sized audience.
You're going to have the church basement-sized audience, but the core of your message isn't going to change

A lot of times my clients seem to be thinking, "Oh,
first, I'm going to grow an audience, and then I'm
going to have my real movement, then I'm going to

.ve my real message." But it actually starts with you having this vision now, in the church basement. The vision doesn't change, your audiences change as you step into the role of leader of that movement. It's you who hasn't shown up yet. Not your people! They are waiting for the messiah to come.

STEP SIX:

ALIGN BELIEFS AND VALUES

The other thing that doesn't change are the values and beliefs that unite your community. In order for people to take action, they need to grasp how you and your movement are not only different but how your tribe is going to help them get to this New Bliss. Let's start by identifying the beliefs that bind your community together. What are their core values? What does everyone in the movement believe? And then, what's that line in the sand that are the nos? I want you to push yourself to be polarizing. There has to be someone who would look at that list of values and say, "Hell, no, that is not for me." Just like you need an enemy, you need to understand what are and aren't your tribe. That helps people identify whether your movement is for them.

One of the best examples I've ever seen of this is Donald Trump's recent presidential campaign. Never mind what your personal opinion is of him; Trump has done a beautiful job of identifying (in a very polarizing way) what the "hell, yes" and "hell, no" values of his community are.

Every time he talks, he uses two words; he uses "we" and "they." So, he doesn't talk about "I," it's: "We're making America great again," and they're—what?—intercepting our borders," or "they're committing crimes," or "they're celebrating planes flying into buildings." Saying "we" and "them" is part of the way he uses language to create a movement of people who are behind making America great again: "We're in this."

It makes those people who aren't supporting Donald Trump the enemy. It's the people who believe in his values, they get what the values are, they're very clear that they're in, and it's very clear who's out. Everyone can really quickly identify as in the circle or out of the circle. He's not being all-inclusive. There's not a big tent, there's a very clear "us versus them."

There has to be a "Yes, we believe this," and a "No, we don't believe that." There have to be insiders and outsiders. For many of you, this will be an area of major resistance because you want to include everyone. I know that might feel good in the conception phase, but when no one is following your movement, it's a lonely road.

I want to change the publishing industry to be more oriented towards long-term service for readers and less oriented to immediate book sales for publisher revenue. I actually believe publishers can make more money, authors can have more control, and readers can get more problems solved—but it requires a major disruption. That's why one of my enemies is the book-writing workshop. But that doesn't mean that I think people who run them are bad. One of the values that's outside my circle is the idea, "Writing is a craft." That's still a very positive value, and it's not a value that I'm against in theory, but it's not part of this movement. I don't want you to just put things outside the circle that are so intensely negative that nobody would get behind them. If you have something outside your circle that's negative, find a way to say it that is positive–perhaps the way somebody from another movement, the book-writing workshop movement, for example, would say it.

STEP SEVEN:
TARGET THE PRIMARY PAIN POINT

As important as it is to know the New Bliss you are driving towards and to know the values of the community, these are attractors but not activators for change. Harvard economics professor N. Gregory Mankiw has a pretty popular theory on what motivates people to change. He posits that consumers are weighing a trade-off between what they have now and the cost of what they want. "This creates an important check on spending power and tends to forcefully prioritize the consumer's spending practices," Mankiw writes. "He first meets his needs before fulfilling non-necessary desires."

What this means to you and your movement is that your New Bliss is a pretty picture, but it will also seem unlikely to come true in the skeptical eyes of consumers, and so committing to this New Bliss will feel like foregoing the sure thing of what they have now for some unnecessary desire for a possible future difference. Said another way, your early adopters just aren't going to believe the risk of the possibility is worth the investment in the vision.

Where does this leave us? Well, what it means is that we need to go back to that shared suffering from step three and identify a trade-off that we can win with our early adopters. I call this the process of targeting the primary pain point.

Martin Luther King, Jr. had a big dream for his community, but there were many more immediate problems that needed to be solved before that dream could become a reality. If we're moving towards the day where "my poor little children will live in a nation where they'll not be judged by the color of their skin but by the content of their character," then we're moving away from segmented schools. So, if I were coaching MLK, what I would be saying to him is, the book we need to write is about why we need to desegregate schools.

The first families that were affected by their kids being bussed to inadequate schools, when they lived next door to a perfectly good school, those were people who might not otherwise be activists. They might not naturally gravitate towards being in the movement to end racial injustice in America. These could be just quiet, everyday citizens, but suddenly, their brilliant daughter who lives next door to an amazing school can't go there, and has to be bussed for five hours a day, two-and-a-half hours each way, to a really crappy school. And so, the "reluctant consumer," who is now so moved to action by the injustice or pain they are facing, is suddenly able to make the trade-off that it's worth it to them to be a part of this movement.

No matter how big or lofty your vision is, your book is going to be about the primary pain point. Kind Bars couldn't start by getting processed foods out of grocery stores. They started with the problem their early adopters had: needing healthy, affordable snacks. Slack couldn't start by running ads to eliminate all email across the globe, so they started with small, tech-savvy, virtual teams who were actively looking for a solution to email overwhelm. Tom's Shoes might want all of us to send money to a developing country every time we shop, but that trade-off is too much to ask for no matter how gorgeous their vision is. And so they offered us cute shoes at a reasonable price, and did the heavy lifting to send shoes to developing communities on our behalf.

When you get specific about the most immediate problem in front of your most likely apostles or early adopters, then you can start to see how you can create a trade-off that is an easy yes for them to get on your vision-train.

My big vision, for instance, is about changing the publishing industry so that it's more fair to authors, better for readers, and more stable for publishers. But going straight to that vision will not help me start a movement. My early adopters are people like you who WANT to make a difference, who NEED to help people in a way that matters.

I know I can get you worked up about not being of service, about your life not being put to use, about the lessons that you've learned not being taken into account when you shape the rest of your life, right? If I say to my community, just write a book and who cares if no one reads it, that wouldn't be enough for them. Over and over again, my clients say to me, "No, this book has to actually help people, I'm not doing it just to hear myself talk." That's where the desire to change just rises to the surface. Solving that problem makes it worth the trade-off to join this movement. (Which I hope you will do if you haven't already!)

In the next chapter we'll talk about your book, and what your book needs to be about to get people to buy and engage. The early adopters are less able to see the future vision that you're building than you are. We need to reverse-engineer the steps to your New Bliss.

So, if we wanted to get to that New Bliss, if we wanted to get to that ideal, what is the next thing that the people who are likely to be a part of this movement will need to take care of? I want you to identify how you want your reader to be different at the end of the book. What is it that you can help them move away from that will allow them to see the bigger vision of what's possible for them?

When we have all that in place, when we know what you are moving toward and what they are moving away from, then what we need is—and this is our big turning point in our journey—an igniting call to adventure. And that's precisely what we'll talk about in the next chapter.

Q: Are we defining things from our perspective or from other people's perspective? Because I think that those are different. I think my people would say one thing and I think something else.

A: You have to define everything from your people's perspective. When you define things from your perspective, you are likely to judge others or make them wrong. One of the things I notice Movement-makers trying, often with little success, is to convince the very people they want to help that they're wrong. When someone comes to me, and they've been trying to write a book for twenty years, I don't say, "The enemy is the choices you made not to get your book done, like going to writers' workshops that encourage the culture of working on a book instead of finishing one." I say, "Of course you went to a writers' workshop, because they're out there and sold you a bill of goods that it was making a difference." So, I don't make our prospects take responsibility for that because that's really making them wrong when I'm trying to get them into our movement. It can't just be that every single one of those people is stupid. I focus more on who might have been preventing them from knowing the information that's our almost God-given right to know.

But it's basically the system that benefits from writers' workshops whose attendees don't know how to make money from their books. They keep down competition and generate income at the same time. The system is doing what it's designed to do, but the system also benefited from not teaching you how to get a book actually finished. So, that's really where I think your power is, it takes away from them being the bad guy, because they made bad decisions, of course they did! Everyone—almost everybody—has made all the same bad decisions.

And it's just like, if you listen to Martin Luther King's "I Have a Dream" speech, you can hear that he's not blaming individual listeners or saying that little black boys and little black girls can't hold hands as brothers and sisters. He's basically saying that this system is rigged so that little black boys and little black girls lose. Of course you're not holding hands, you're not even allowed to go to the same school!

CHAPTER THREE

CREATING THE RIGHT BOOK TO IGNITE YOUR MOVEMENT

"YOU NEVER CHANGE THINGS BY
FIGHTING THE EXISTING REALITY.
TO CHANGE SOMETHING, BUILD A
NEW MODEL THAT MAKES THE EXISTING
MODEL OBSOLETE."

R. BUCKMINSTER FULLER

In this chapter, we are going to talk about how to create an igniting call to adventure for your movement. There are lots of ways to kick off a movement, but the way we are going to create that igniting call to adventure—because it's probably more fun than a bomb blast or a tornado—is with a book and with a book launch.

One of the ways your book can be more than just a solution to a problem—more than, say, a *"For Dummies"* book, has to do with you and the relationship your reader has with you. You can build that relationship by establishing yourself as the hero of the journey to discover this New Bliss we're headed for.

STEP EIGHT
ENGINEER YOUR HERO'S JOURNEY

I want you to think about how you came to lead this movement through the lens of what I like to think of as the reluctant hero. A reluctant hero is an ordinary person who requires motivation to start the cycle of the hero.

That is part of how we'll answer the question: "Who are you to lead this movement?" When you tell your story as the reluctant hero, that's also the story of all of the people in your movement. You say, "Hey, I didn't want to have to learn how to solve this problem, but that's the hand I was dealt."

What you want to do is create a story that starts with where you were before the "call to adventure." Joseph Campbell calls this "the ordinary world." This is where you were back before you found your movement. Describe your life and what it was like before you discovered your movement.

Your next step is describing the call to adventure. For me, that was the moment when I went to a writer's workshop, and I noticed that there were a lot of people talking about writing but not very many people actually getting books done. While I was there, I realized that these people really needed someone to lead them. I just didn't think that it could be me. So, in the ordinary world, you have the call to adventure, that first idea, and then you have the refusal of the call.

"The hero may refuse the adventure or deny the ability to move beyond the status quo. The heralded event may even be ignored—all of these constitute the 'Refusal of the Call.' The use of magical intervention is then needed to plunge the hero into the unknown. The reluctant hero requires supernatural forces to urge him on, while the willing adventurer gathers amulets (magical items) and advice from the protector as aid for the journey."
~ Joseph Campbell, *The Hero with a Thousand Faces.*

I was at that writer's workshop because I wanted someone to help me write a book, but everyone at the workshop was looking to me to help *them*. Reluctantly, I did, but only because of a series of serendipities and synchronicities that lead to many of the attendees of that workshop asking me to solve their problems.

The next step in the Hero's Journey is "meeting with the mentor." This happened to me when I went to this book-writing workshop in October, and then two months later met Jack Canfield from the *Chicken Soup for the Soul* series. That's when I had a nervous breakdown, because I realized just how hard this was going to be. I suddenly understood why publishers were doing things the way they were doing them, because doing it another way would be really, really hard. In fact, my mentor even tried to talk me out of it because it would be so hard. He told me exactly what I had to do and then basically challenged me to see if I was strong enough to cross the threshold.

Okay, so that is the end of act one, which happens in the ordinary world. This is where your people are now, so it's very important to describe this with the eyes you had before you went on the rest of your adventure.

Once you cross the threshold, you are in a special world. A world your people won't really be able to see yet, so it's important for you to keep them in mind as you describe what happened. The special world is where your movement is being formed, and it's that special bubble that you are in and you can take your people to visit. Joseph Campbell talks about tests and allies and enemies you meet after you accept the call. Then comes the approach to the inmost cave. That is the big moment, the moment I talk about where you decide if you're going to go all in or not. For me, that test was when I got a really, really, really good job offer, and my business wasn't completely working. It was too successful to quit, but not successful enough to pay all of my bills, which was a heavy situation to be in.

So I got a job offer, and it was a dream job at a great location—it was everything I would have wanted in my corporate days. I had to really go into that inner-most cave and decide if I just wanted to play it safe and have a paycheck, or if I really wanted to create this movement.

After the inner-most cave decision, there is an ordeal. This is the turning point for your movement. The ordeal for me was when I said "no" to that job. I had to make a decision about how much I believed in this movement and how much I was going to put behind it, and that's when I launched the current program, the way it is now. I had to make a huge investment in my business, and I had to really change my orientation from *thinking* I was service-oriented to really stepping up into what it means to serve.

The reward comes from seizing the sword. Only after you seize the sword for yourself can you start on the road back to the ordinary world, and return with the magic elixir to the ordinary world with your lessons won. For me, when I reached this point, my messaging changed, my movement grew, and I was able to come back and say, "Look, guys, I thought about playing it safe, I thought about taking the traditional job, but you guys and this message mean too much to me, this movement means too much to me to just walk away."

I want you to tell your story as the hero's journey, looking for the symbols and the language to inspire connection and action. My business uses a feather. It's one of the big symbols that I use that drives our connection: everybody gets a feather when they graduate, they see feathers on my book cover, and the painting I had commissioned. For me, the feather is permission to fly, to rise up, to conquer your goals. I normally use this rainbow fade color, coming into focus I always use terms like "start a movement" and "make a difference" consistently throughout the language, and those are all part of how we're building that movement and how we're joining people together.

What are the symbols? What's the language that would resonate with the beliefs and that "I Have a Dream" speech that you wrote? Are there any images that come out of that speech, any symbols, any colors, anything that we can really use to start to visualize this movement?

STEP NINE:
DRAW TOGETHER YOUR INFLUENCERS

The next thing that I want you to do is identify the influencers who can help bring attention to your cause and think about how we can bring them into the fold and empower them to help grow this movement. One of the ways you're going to ignite the call to adventure is not just by having the book launch, but by having other people, these influencers, involved and excited about your book. Who are the people that would be most excited about your movement, and most interested in supporting that movement? Who could you write about within your group?

As we start to talk about crafting your book in the next chapter, I want you to identify who we can include in your book.

For instance, with your launch you are going to have some sort of giveaway, but that giveaway doesn't have to be all yours. Are there other people from whom you can assemble a package of stuff that supports your movement? There might be people who would be excited to support your book and to give you, let's say, something free that will be part of the download that comes with the book.

Who is not competitive with you but reaches the same audience? Let's say your movement is for new moms and you're a baby sleep coach. Formula companies and diaper companies are both reaching your new mom and are not competing with you. Can we work them into your client conversion book? Are your values aligned? How could we make connections now with the people who would most likely want to promote your book because they wouldn't feel competitive and they're 100% on mission? If every value that you have in the center of your circle is shared with them, your ideal reader is shared with them, and you're not competing with them, they are a good target to become one of your influencers.

When you tell stories about influencers in your book, they are more likely to spread the word and become influencers for your movement. Who are the influencers you could write about so that they become influencers for your movement? We do all of this before we outline the book, before we write the book, before we even know what the book is about, even before we really know what our igniting moment is going to be. We want to figure out how can we incorporate these influencers into the process—a step, frankly, that most people don't really think about, leaving them asking for praise or testimonials only after their book is done. If you think about them while you're forming your movement, you give yourself the chance to ask what you can do for them right now. Thinking it through ahead of time is going to help find the right influencers to incorporate into the book.

STEP TEN:
BAM! CREATE YOUR IGNITING
CALL TO ADVENTURE

An igniting call to adventure is the moment when your movement coalesces, where it goes from being an idea in your head, maybe with some of your friends and family supporting it, to an actual thing that we can objectively measure and say whether or not it's working.

The way that I recommend igniting your call to adventure is with a book launch. You need a reason for people to pay attention to you. Now, Jesus had something come in handy here, you may be familiar with the crucifixion, so that was quite convenient. There are other ways to ignite the call to adventure. The Sandy Hook shooting was one for the gun control movement. For some people, it can be a speaking event. Think about when the iPhone came out, and Steve Jobs presented it at MacWorld in his black turtleneck. That was sort of a pivotal moment that happened in our culture. There are certainly many moments like this on election nights or campaign speeches that can be an igniting event.

One of the most powerful aspects of having a book to ignite the call to adventure is that it is an engineered experience that you can create a launch around, and you can use that book launch as a rallying cry. And that book needs to transform your readers' belief of what's possible. It also, quite handily, makes you the only possible leader of your movement.

Your book will balance what your reader is moving away from with helping them to see what New Bliss is possible. Both sides—the top-down and bottom-up—are equally important, but the "envelope" of your book, that is the label on the cover which will tell your reader whether or not the book is for them, needs to highlight the problem they are moving away from. That's where we focus the title and the marketing, but we can pull them along further once they are bought in.

Using those influencers we identified, we're now going to build their message right into the book. Your book is going to do a couple of things. It's going to kick off this movement, and it's going to fund the movement in the short term. We'll talk about how to write a book that kicks off your movement in the next chapter, and then in Chapter Five, we'll go deep on how you can use that book to fund your movement.

INSIDE THE AUTHOR INCUBATOR
On Competition

Q: How do I find influencers where there are synergies and who feel completely on board with my message, but who aren't competitors?

A: The trick is to think about what you have to offer them. For instance, let's say you want the Ritz Carlton to be an influencer and they have recently renovated a hotel. Let's say that in your chapter you were talking about planning your office, or why your office space matters as an entrepreneur. Maybe you could ask to interview the Ritz's interior designer and they could talk about the importance of place and how they create the hotel's environment, which would help them promote their new decorating scheme. Think about ways that you can build them into the book. It could be something as simple as just putting a quote

from something they've already written in
We want them to get that "this is the mo
building and I would love for you to be a
movement, I would love you to lend your voice to
that movement."

When you ask them to promote your book on launch
day, you're not asking them to promote you, you're
just the reluctant hero of this movement.

CHAPTER FOUR

ARCHITECTING YOUR MISSION

"MAKE NO LITTLE PLANS; THEY HAVE
NO MAGIC TO STIR MEN'S
BLOOD AND PROBABLY THEMSELVES
WILL NOT BE REALIZED."

DANIEL BURNHAM

Be honest. Do you need money to fund your movement? Your first priority, if you really have that servant's heart, is to create a movement that can be sustained. Even the most important movement in the world can't run on hope and good ideas alone. Funding your movement could mean paying your bills, it could mean paying for branding to help get the message positioned right in the market, it could mean paying for advertising to get people to sign your petition, or paying for publishing and marketing services for your book.

If you want a book that not only ignites your movement but funds it, there are really two types of books that you can write. If you're looking to grants, donations, maybe micro-loans or investment capital as the way your movement is going to get funded, then I recommend a **list-building book**. When other people are footing the bill for your movement, because your movement serves people who aren't going to pay you, then we really want to grow your platform and your position as quickly as possible. (A clever exception here is the Tom's Shoes story, because in that case, the movement is for people who couldn't pay–the shoeless underprivileged. But in order to fund that movement, they converted clients who *could* pay–consumers who want cute shoes. So you might consider this model if your movement similarly serves non-buyers.)

If the people who you help with your book could be further helped by working directly with you, and they would invest in themselves to be a part of this movement and get the results that being a part of this movement would give them, then I recommend a **client conversion book**. Converting clients includes things like teaching classes, running workshops, working one-on-one with people, selling products—anything where you will make money from people who would likely benefit from this movement.

Maybe you have a trust fund or a well-paying full-time job and are in the enviable position of not needing money to fuel your movement, then you can consider a **platform-speaking book**. Remember, you will still need to be able to make some investments, like in a PR person or in branding, marketing, social media, and video, but if you can do that without collecting money from other people, then getting media and speaking opportunities—even if they are unpaid—can be a great approach to grow your movement organically.

Many people think they have a great idea to combine these three ideas and write a book that gets them everything: speaking gig, press, a big mailing list, and lots of clients. Sadly, this approach, which has been tested time and time again, is a guaranteed path to failure. Trying to do everything with your book consistently leads to sub-par results. But focusing on one of those three approaches will allow you to actually reap benefits far beyond that goal. It's counter-intuitive I know, but trying to do everything get you a mish mash of unpredictable, unrepeatable, unscalable and hard-to-quantify results. Doing only one thing not only gets you that one thing, but it also gets you a bunch of bonuses and side benefits. We are rewarded for clarity and constraint.

Once you pick the type of book you need to write, it's time to start creating. My biggest piece of advice here is, "Don't start by writing!" In fact, in my Difference Process™ there are six steps before you reach the writing part of the journey. For more on this, you can read my book, *The Difference: 10 Steps to Writing a Book that Matters*, but I'm going to recap the highlights of the ten steps in case you missed them. (Oh, and if you want a free copy of that book, email me at Angela@ TheAuthorIncubator.com and I'll send it over!)

DEFINE YOUR IDEAL READER

Back in Step Two, we talked about noticing your apostles and likely early adopters. The ideal reader of your book doesn't come from the mainstream. Your movement is not going to be launched and then accepted by everyone it could help. First it will be accepted by those apostles we talked about.

This idea is based on the *Diffusion of Innovation* studies ignited by the work of Everett Rogers, who first wrote the book on this topic in 1962. What Rogers explains is the way new ideas or products are accepted into use. All the way on the left of this graphic are the 2.5% of people who are innovators. This is where your apostles will come from. Next are the early adopters. These are the 13.5% of people who might not otherwise want your book or your movement, but because you are going to Target the Primary Pain Point with your book, these people have a good chance of becoming followers of your movement. Everyone else represented on this chart—that's 84% of people on the planet—they are not for you. Not with this book, anyway!

Most authors target the middle of the curve you see below. They say things like "everyone needs self-love," or "this book is for all kinds of people, there's something for everyone."

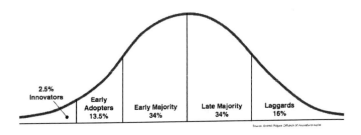

The truth is, something for everyone means nothing for no one, because if you target the majority, they simply won't be able to see you and hear you. You will be invisible to them.

When we identify your ideal reader, we need to look in this first 16% for the one person who is so in pain and so needing to heal that they are ready to try something different.

Your ideal reader is the person who needs to move away from this pain point more than anyone else. There are lots of people your work could help, but think of the people that need this the most. Pick one of them and create a profile. Your ideal reader isn't "women 35–45 going through a transition." I want it to be a very specific person. So, it's "Mary, who lives in Chicago, has two kids, works as a lawyer, and her husband just left her for a 22-year-old paralegal."

Can you see already how Mary is set up to become the reluctant hero we discussed in step 8? Could you write her hero's journey from the ordinary world where she is now to what it will be after she joins your movement?

Go into the future for your ideal reader, let's say two years from now, and tell the story of how they got your book and they joined your movement, they came to see you speak or they signed up for your program. You were the guru that they met along the way that made them go all in. How did your ideal reader become the hero: by reading your book and going through this process with you?

IDENTIFY YOUR VOICE

The next step is identify your voice, and your voice is very specific to being the leader of this movement. If you're a leader of the movement and you are looking to coach or run workshops, you want to make sure that you are approachable and similar to the way you would be as a coach. You want to sound like you would sound when you are coaching.

If you're looking to speak as the primary outcome from the book, your voice needs to really focus on storytelling, so you don't have to be the one solving the problem, you have to be the one seeing the problem. Malcolm Gladwell and Elizabeth Gilbert are great examples of this. In both cases, you're probably not going to hire either of them to be your coach or to solve the problem of, let's say, creativity or making quick decisions, but what they do and the roles they serve in our culture are to point out the problems more clearly through storytelling. Then they leave it to us coaches and consultants out there to actually solve those problems.

If you're a speaker, you're the observer of the problem in a way that's new and unique that will help other people solve it, but it's not that you're going to give a list of solutions, it's really about seeing it in a new way. Let's say you want to "revolutionize the legal industry." If you want to be a speaker, you are really going to focus on seeing the problem, and then the people who are going to solve the problem are the people who paid you to speak: the HR department or CEO or the partners who hire you. Your role is to help get everyone onboard with their vision—what they're really going to pay you for is getting everyone to see the problem in their way. This is almost the opposite of what your voice would be if you were writing a client conversion book. With a client conversion book, you need them to see the problem AND the path to a viable solution because you are the person to solve it.

With list building, on the other hand, it's all about community and "I'm one of you." Your voice needs to really be that "we have a dream" focus. I think a great example here is the "Occupy Wall Street" movement. That was really about the" we," so much so that there wasn't even a clear leader. The "we" is very important with a list-building book, and so is building tribe.

Your book is a love letter from you to your ideal reader. You need to know who you are in that relationship and how you want that relationship to develop. The type of book and the outcome you want from your book influences that, but your voice, first and foremost, has to come across as you NOW being the person you want to be to your reader in the future.

FRAME YOUR OUTCOME

What is the evidence we need to gather so we'll know you have started a movement?

Everything in your being will tell you to skip this step and to ask for as much as possible of whatever it is you want. The Universe, however, doesn't know how to respond to these commands. How are we going to know if what you are doing is working if we don't have actual bench marks to measure against? We might quit when things are actually working, or we might think they are working when they are not and miss an opportunity to course-correct. Without these milestones, there will be no way to tell if you have actually started a movement or not.

You have already identified the type of book you want to write (client conversion, list-building or platform speaking). Now we just have to put a number on that. Look twelve months into the future. If you're writing a list-building book, how many people do you want on your list? That could be any list: Facebook "likers" or followers, Twitter, Periscope, email, etc. What's the number of followers in one place that you would like?

For client conversion books, what is the revenue you would like to generate from products related to your book in a year? My general recommendation for funding a movement is starting around the $10,000 per month mark within 90 days, and closer to $20,000 or $30,000 a month within a year.

With a platform-speaking book, what are the number of speaking engagements you want to do in a year? Think about your time and how much travel can you do, realistically, in twelve months. How much, in a year, could you do media? Media will often include travel, but it just might include blocking off big parts of your day. What's the budget that you have for this stuff? If you were looking at spending $5,000 a month with a PR person, you could easily be doing four media engagements a week. Could you handle that?

FOCUS YOUR AUTHOR MOJO

Focus Your Author Mojo is really about preparing yourself to create that igniting call to adventure. This isn't just a paper you are turning in for English class. An Igniting Call to Adventure is a book that is written from flow and with Source as a co-creator. The book needs to be written quickly and it needs to be inspired. How do you do that? Well, your responsibility isn't to DO it as much as it is for creating the conditions for Source/God/whatever-you-call-it to come through you by creating the best possible conditions to write.

What time of day are you most effective writing?

How long do you like to write in a single session that gives you the best results?

What are the things you need to do to support your inner author? Is it a cup of tea? A fuzzy pair of pants or socks?

What are the things that are going to make you most comfortable?

Thinking back to past projects, what were the times that were most productive? Was it on deadline? How can we set up tighter deadlines? Was it when you were more relaxed? How can we spread that writing out so it's more relaxed?

Decluttering is a big piece of this for a lot of people. Will being in a cluttered space slow down your writing or block the muses? For most people, the answer is yes.

Create a writing plan where your inner author can come out. Schedule your writing time. If you're really good for two days locked in a room, schedule those two days. If you want to write an hour a day, every day, put that on your calendar. Making your author mojo a priority helps create a space for your inner author to come out. That's when you're writing in flow.

ENVISION YOUR SUCCESS

Picture how successful your movement will be two years from today. If you were someone who was leading that movement, what would you be doing? Would you be registering your business as a nonprofit or charity? Would you be dressing differently? Where would you live? Would the leader of that movement be running around with a cracked iPhone screen and a purse full of melted M&Ms? Does your wardrobe match what somebody who's running this movement would dress like? Are there ways that you would be acting differently, as the already successful leader of this movement? How can you (even symbolically) start living like that now and not wait 'til the movement is done?

RELEASE YOUR BLOCKS

Everything that stands between you and the completed book happens in the outline. When your outline is aligned with the outcomes you want for your movement and the pain your ideal reader is moving away from, we, at The Author Incubator, call that an "inline."

That's why we call the step of creating your inline the release-your-blocks step. This is where you have freed your inner author and you are ready to craft a love letter from you to your ideal reader.

Remember the Primary Pain Point? Everything in this inline has to take them to resolution of that immediate pain. The question I often ask my authors is, "How do you want your reader to be at the end of this book?" Frame up that problem so they know exactly what they have to do to get it solved.

If you're writing a client conversion book, the way you want your reader to be different at the end of the book is this: at the end of the book, the reader will know how to resolve that Primary Pain Point and they will know they can do it on their own, but they will be faster and have less trial and error if they do it with you. In your outline, everything needs to lead to that realization. One way that I recommend to do that is to take them through your hero's journey so they can see how that can be THEIR hero's journey too.

The most important step in this process—and the one most authors want to skip—is getting super-honest about what the problem is in the ordinary world. Now, this "ordinary world" concept is really important for you to get, because the way your readers are describing the problem is NOT going to be how you will describe the problem now that you are on the other side of it. But you have to get to the question they're asking, at the beginning of the book, in the ordinary world. Now, we've already gone through our hero's journey, so we know about the special world, but we have to return to the ordinary world with the elixir.

Your entire first chapter—possibly your first two chapters—need to be in that ordinary world, defining that problem and confronting them with that: that moment, that opportunity to go into the special world with you. Your introduction and Chapter One, maybe even Chapter Two, are going to be in the ordinary world. Then we can give them the call to move into the special world. That's where we're going to give them the steps, that's where we're going to give them the problems and the obstacles they will face in the special world once they cross the threshold.

You can even acknowledge that they're probably going to refuse the call because it doesn't sound very fun. You can write about when you refused the call, and about why you decided to go all in with this movement. You want to cross the threshold with them. I talk about this as the join-up with them, you want to have that "join up" moment before you take them into the special world.

The chapters in the special world need to show them the obstacles they're going to face. I like the structure of five or six steps, and then a chapter on obstacles. You are the guru, you're the person who they met on the road, so you want to show up as that leader for them through the dark and treacherous path. You don't want to expect that they'll just get it. You want them to know that there are going to be challenges and obstacles, and you want to prepare them for those challenges and obstacles. What's going to come up along the way?

Here's where you put in client stories, if you have them, or examples of when somebody who had your help was able to overcome the obstacles that are going to come up. Don't pretend this is easy. When you get to the end of that process, to the resolution, that is really your conclusion. What do you want your reader to do next, what's going to happen next? I'm leaving you here on the road, what's the message I want you to take with you? Be the sage, and leave them with advice if they're not going to continue working with you.

Tell your reader in that concluding chapter what their best way is for moving forward, now that they know this stuff. That might be recommending they get a mentor, even if it's not you. That might be recommending that they have support systems or accountability. What are the things they're going to need?

Go gather research, if there is anything you aren't ready to write. What I recommend is having somewhere between eight and ten things that you're going to write about in each of those chapters. You should look at each of those things in each chapter and know what they are before you start writing. When you know what's in each of your chapters, you have released your blocks.

ESTABLISH YOUR AUTHOR FEELING STATE

Once you've released your blocks, you can finally move on to the next step, which is where you will write. What you want to do first is write stream-of-conscious style for thirty minutes. You can do this by setting a timer for thirty minutes and writing about "why I'm starting this movement." Whatever happens, don't pick your pen up from the page or your fingers up off the keyboard. So, even if all you're saying is, "I don't know what I should be typing now, but I'm still typing," I just want you to type for thirty minutes. At the end of that thirty minutes, I want you to get your word count and double it. If your 30-minute test produced 750 words, you would double that to establish your writing rate as 1500 words per hour. This will be an important metric for us later.

When you sit down to write, I want you to identify where you are on the Author Feeling State Scale. The Author Feeling State Scale runs from negative ten to positive ten.

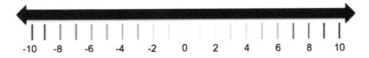

If you are in the negative numbers, you're not writing, you're blocked. You have a writing appointment in your calendar, but words are not going onto the page. If you are anywhere between a positive one and ten, you can write and words are coming onto the paper, but when you are writing between a positive one and a positive five, it feels like you are writing a paper for college. Words are coming out but it's not fun. It's a struggle. If you looked at your word count per hour, it would be at least 20% lower than the word count from your writing test.

If you are writing between 80% and 200% of your words-per-hour rate, then you're in a state of flow. You are somewhere between six and ten on the Author Feeling State scale. If your standard rate is 1500 wph and you are writing, say, 3000 wph, you are at ten on the scale. If your standard rate is 1500 wph and you are writing, say, 1200 wph, you are at a six on the scale. And if your standard rate is 1500 wph and you are writing 500 wph, you are probably at a three on the scale.

To create an igniting call to adventure, we want to write as much of your book in a six to ten author feeling state as possible. That means you are writing in flow, that means you were inspired, touched by the muses, really connected with your ideal reader, and that's where we get the most usable work, so the most word count that gets used, the fewest rewrites and your most powerful voice.

When you sit down to write and identify that you're in a negative author feeling state, our first job is to get you into positive territory. This counts as part of your writing assignment for that day. If you are somewhere between one and five, you're going to be writing below your standard rate. You can do that—that's how you wrote most of your papers in college—and you will finish that way. But if we want the best chance at starting a movement, we want to take time at this point to see if we can elevate you on the scale. The most important thing is for you to make a conscious decision about is to either write or stop writing and move yourself up the scale.

There are a bunch of things that you can do to get yourself into a place that is going to create a book and ignite call to adventure, not just pound out an academic paper. Some of those things might be physical movement, coaching, visualization, aromatherapy, creating a ritual as a writer, "throat-clearing" exercises where you're just journaling, and body work, just to name a few. When I'm working with an author, I find where they are on the scale and tailor an exercise to move them up if that's what's needed.

As you do this work to move yourself up the scale, don't think, "I'm procrastinating," don't think, "I'm doing this wrong." Think instead, "This is exactly what doing this right looks like. This is how the pros do it. Here I am at a five, I could write and get word count out, but I'm going to make a decision instead to go organize my sock drawer, or call the person I was supposed to call last night that's distracting me from my mission." Go do that other thing and when you come back, check where you are on the author feeling state scale.

Let's say you were writing 500 wph. You go do other work, come back, and now you're at a seven or eight and you're writing back at your standard rate of 1500 wph. You can see how it works. In scenario one, you write for two hours at 500 wph for 1000 total words. In scenario two you write for 30 minutes and get 250 words. Then you take thirty minutes off, so 0 words. And then you come back and write 1500 words in the second hour. Your total word count in scenario two is 1750 words—almost twice scenario one, and it was more pleasant for you and probably better for the reader. So yes, pushing yourself to slog through can work, but what I find is that addressing the obstacles to being in that state of flow ends up maximizing your productivity and effectiveness.

This is the math of creating an igniting call to adventure with your book. You need to be a 100% committed to writing in flow. That means sometimes not writing when you have it scheduled in order to move yourself into that space where the muses can visit, inspiration can come, and your creativity is freed.

NURTURE YOUR MANUSCRIPT

During the writing phase, it's always best to keep writing forward. Don't look back and rewrite until you get to the end. Then you can focus on nurturing the manuscript. This is the time for substantial edits and rewrites. This is also the time when you will work on the design, the front and back material like your bio, acknowledgements and dedication, and the marketing copy. You can also use this period to get advance praise for your book or even a forward. Make sure you are working with an editor and designer who understand your "New Bliss" and how this Primary Pain Point fits into the bigger picture. Also make sure they understand the type of book you are trying to write and what success looks like.

Most manuscripts are poorly nurtured because the editor and designer compete with each other and with the author, pulling the book in different directions. Most designers want to make a book cover that's beautiful. That's not a BAD goal, but it should take a back seat to whatever your primary outcome is. Most editors are trained and committed to making your book "English Class Good" but good enough for an A in English does not tell us if it's good enough to get you clients or speaking engagements or folks signed up for your list. Make sure your whole team is marching to the same beat and remember that you are the anointed leader—you must lead your team on behalf of your people.

CREATE YOUR MASTERPIECE

All right, step number nine is to create your masterpiece. This step is about making sure you publish in the right way. It's important that you have a publisher who's going to support your bigger vision, not just the book and book sales.

With traditional publishing, the author sells the right to exploit the intellectual property of the book, generally for 90 percent of author earnings. The problem is that the author is now in conflict with the publisher, because the author can't afford to advertise their own book (since they are taking such a small piece of the profits) and the publisher wants to prevent the author from selling other, similar products or services that might compete with the book. So the author is hog-tied and unable to grow their business beyond that tiny share of book sales. What's more, the publisher will often change the direction of the book, the layout, and even the cover if they think it will gain more buyers. Their goal, after all, is book sales.

Self-publishing avoids that problem by giving authors all the power in their own hands. The problem is that authors have to learn all the aspects of publishing such as editing, distribution, layout, and cover design. If you don't know what you're doing, the results can look like amateurish. Worse, most authors who publish this way don't get the front-end impact of book sales (because they don't know how to sell books like a traditional publisher) and they also lose the back-end impact of book sales because they don't know how to write a book that generates long term revenue. Sadly, self-publishing is another kind of lose-lose.

With custom or hybrid publishing, there is a broad spectrum of options from awesome to terrible. What I recommend is finding a publisher who knows how to design and sell books and who will understand and support your other outcomes as well and not block you. What this means is that you want to pay for the publishing services, because the alternative—not paying—means you lose control, and the alternative of paying less and doing it yourself means you don't get the outcome for your book that you deserve. Find a partner who focuses on the outcome and can get your book where it needs to go. A book, in my opinion, is too big of a thing to risk doing it yourself and doing it wrong—especially if it's intended to ignite the call to adventure for your early adopters.

EXPAND YOUR REACH

Step ten is where we go beyond the book and put the marketing plan into action. What's your launch going to be? How are you going to include those influencers in the process? This could be setting up guest blog posts or booking yourself on podcasts, as examples. How are we going to go beyond the book? What's the next thing the reader can sign up for with you?

So, all that stuff is happening in the "create your masterpiece" step.

Your message needs to be visible, and we need to find those early adopters for you to really create an igniting call to adventure and not just a book that could make a difference if the right people picked it up. Following these ten steps to create an igniting call to adventure is the difference between having a brilliant idea that could change the world, that could start a movement, and having an idea that's brilliant and that people in the ordinary world can see.

INSIDE THE AUTHOR INCUBATOR
On Who to Write For

Q: How can I focus on one topic when there's so much I want to write about?

A: There are many books to come, but right now we need to find your twelve apostles. Imagine you're Jesus and you've got this plan, you've got to convert the Jews into being Christians and tell them you're the Messiah—you're not going for everyone.

If you got twelve clients at $10,000–$20,000 each from this book, I would call that a success. To me, a success is doing what will fuel your next book and will fund your movement. We don't have to look for thousands of people to read the book; we are looking for those first clients, because that's what will really build that movement. Those are the people in some kind of an immediate, painful situation that's causing them to reach out for your help. Most authors in transformation are so focused on being broad that they're trying to serve the middle of the bell curve. Those people are like Jesus preaching to an elderly couple going to pick up produce at the market. Now, would they say, "Hey, let's hang out with him and the rabbis!" No, they wouldn't, and that's fine, but that's the target who most people are writing their book for. Most people show up and try to write their book for the middle of the bell curve, leaving OUT the 16% of people on the far left of the curve who need it most. The question to ask yourself now is: how can I make an impact and get measurable results that prove I'm building a movement?

CHAPTER FIVE

FUNDING YOUR MOVEMENT

"IT IS NOT THE MOUNTAIN WE CONQUER
BUT OURSELVES."

EDMUND HILLARY

Most people don't have some sort of magical bankroll that is going to make their vision happen. There are lots of missions that are built on fundraising, and that is one way to do it. There are people with trust funds who are happy to spend them down in service to a mission. Both of those options work, but my specialty is helping people who need to bankroll their own movement. The first step in funding your movement is admitting this cold, hard truth.

Without funding, your movement will fail and you will help no one.

Funding your movement is essential, because otherwise you won't get to have a movement. Part of what you do with that funding is pay yourself. Getting clear on how much money you need, whether it's to pay your bills or to pay for advertising for the movement, is essential. Now, I'm not saying that you have to go take this money and buy a yacht, but that may be part of how you fund your movement. You have anointed yourself as the leader of this movement. That makes you the executive director, and the executive director is not going to be very effective if she isn't getting paid.

We want our executive director to have a great salary, because they're never going to give this mission all of their attention if they're worried about paying their bills. If you were hiring someone to run this movement, would you start by looking for a free college intern? Would you want to entrust your movement to somebody who would work for $0—$10,000 a year? No! Let's get somebody who we pay a $150,000 or

$200,000 to run this movement, because you're going to get their full attention.

I nominate you.

What do we need to pay you to get your full, dedicated effort so you don't want to quit your job because you have toxic boss named "you"? All right, so, how are we going to do that?

Part of how we'll set your funding goal is by honestly assessing what you need to live on, and what the movement needs to survive. Do you need to pay for certain staff members or supplies? What do we need to make, per month, for this movement to stay in business with its doors open?

I volunteered, for many years, for an organization that helped me out of a domestic violence situation. They were funded by grants, and when the grants got pulled, they just shut their doors. That's it. Unfunded movement = no movement. They were the only domestic violence agency in D.C. that was need-blind. I had a corporate job, so I wouldn't have been able to get help from the other agencies. Luckily my case was just about finished when they closed, but if I were to find myself in the same situation today, I'd be out of luck. There is no organization that exists to help non-impoverished survivors of domestic violence in Washington, D.C. Why? Because they did not properly fund their movement.

I'm not okay with that!

You may think that funding your movement is for you, and very often, how we talk about it in terms of monthly revenue. This can make it feel like this is your business and you should charge what you are worth and enjoy vacations in sunny places. But the truth is, I come to this with a servant's heart, and without funding, there's no way to get the message out about self-care; there's no way to help people get the message out about how to find out who you are; there's no way to figure out if they can reach their potential. There's no way to move your message forward if you don't have your movement funded. If you aren't willing to do this work, what that tells me is that you are happier to see your people go without help then to do the work required and get the help required to figure this out.

IDENTIFY THE MILESTONES

To get started, we need to know how to measure success. Identify what your monthly income needs to be for your movement. Start by making a list of all your costs. Now I know you don't know all your costs, and it's easy to try to skip this stuff, but if you don't know your actual number, your brain won't be able to help you figure out how to hit that number.

Here are some things you might want to think about as you are trying to find your number.

Your Salary

How much do you need to make to pay your rent or mortgage, your utilities, car payments, groceries, gas, insurance, phone, and other living essentials?

Business Licenses, Legal Fees, and Business Insurance

Plan to spend at least a couple hundred dollars to get your movement properly registered and insured and to get whatever contracts or legal insurance you need to protect your assets.

Equipment and Supplies

Maybe you already have a computer and a printer, but I'd keep a budget aside for replacement equipment and maintenance even if you do.

Advertising and Promotion

You'll need a website and some branding work and it's likely you'll need to pay for advertising. Plan to spend about 20% of what you earn in marketing costs.

Employee Expenses

Whether you are planning to use contractors or wage employees, make a list of who you need to hire and how much you want to budget to fill those roles. Many people hire administrative assistants, marketing managers, account representatives, sales people, designers, and technical workers.

Technological Expenses

Budget a couple hundred dollars for systems like your ecommerce system, your email system, your schedul-

ing software, and other apps and tools to help you run
your business.

Supplies & Postage

You will undoubtedly need to buy some office supplies
and possibly some gifts for clients and team members.
You'll want to save money for paper, pens, printer ink,
and prezzies as well as the postage to stick those pres-
ents in the mail!

Taxes

Don't forget to save some for Uncle Sam!

I once worked for a company who had a CFO named
Bessy Ziannis. Bessy looked like the glamorous movie
star Charlize Theron, and so when I remember this
story, it's always me and Charlize hashing it out in my
mind. Bessie was the CFO when I had my first senior
role in an organization, and she made me do this
bottom-up budget for my business unit which truly
seemed impossible. I'm pretty sure she was getting
frustrated with me for arguing over every line item.

"Look," I said, "we haven't even started this division, I have no idea how much everything costs, and no idea how much we're going to make."

Charlize...er...um...Bessie looked at me with all seriousness and she said, "I bet, if you do this for me, we will be within ten percent when we come to our quarterly check-in." Sure enough, the quarter came up, we looked at my numbers and there it was. I projected just 12% less than our actual expenses and I was only 3% off our total sales.

Everything in your brain will insist that this is an impossible exercise, but it works the OPPOSITE of how you think it does. When you complete this bold act of service to your movement, you are setting an intention for what you will spend and earn in the next year. The power in those intentions can't be under-estimated.

Real businesses, like Apple, or Foot Locker, or Orange Julius even, they don't say "Hey! Let's see what we can make this quarter and hope it's less than we spend!" They put an actual number on their costs and an actual goal for their revenue and then (here's the magic bit, so listen up) then they make DECISIONS to make these expectations come true—or at least close to true.

You can ballpark this. You can take a guess at what you need to live and keep this movement rolling. This is what I learned from that day in Bessie's office and I have never forgotten it. When you estimate or guess what you think things are going to cost, even things you don't know, you will then set to work at making them a reality. If we don't have a number we're going for, we're not going to have the milestone to know whether we're building this movement.

How do we know if we're building this movement?

That's one of the big questions I want us to be able to answer.

Part of why you will want to resist answering this question is because money brings up all sorts of issues. When that happens, I want you to remember the reason you are doing this. You are doing this to SERVE and in order to serve, yes, you will need to eat and buy highlighters. When you remember that you're doing this for a reason beyond yourself, when you have those moments that make you want to quit, you will remember that who you're really quitting on are the people you're supposed to be helping. If that's still tripping you up, please go see a money coach and work through this, because your people deserve for you to get over this and show them the change you know is possible.

This is the thing I have learned in five years in business: that most people, even people who have finished their books with me, quit on their vision. That's really what happens, it looks like they're quitting on their taxes. It looks like they just couldn't make Facebook advertising work. But really, what they were saying is, "I don't really want to help those people that much. I don't really want to make a difference that much, in this way."

YOU NEED TO FEEL THIS FIRST

I met Katie Meyler a few weeks ago on a cruise. She looked like most of the other cruise passengers: sundress, sunglasses on the top of her head, and freckles.

We were sitting in the auditorium of the ship waiting for John Legend to take the stage. Katie told me how she grew up on welfare thinking she was poor and then she went to Haiti and realized she wasn't poor at all. When she came back to the U.S., she started the More Than Me Foundation to give girls in Liberia the opportunity to go to school instead of prostituting themselves on the streets in exchange for clean drinking water. Katie now works to overhaul Liberia's entire education system alongside the Ministry of Education.

In September, 2013, she, alongside Nobel Laureate and Liberian President Ellen Johnson Sirleaf, cut the ribbon for the More Than Me Academy—the first tuition-free, all-girls school in Liberia. More recently, Katie was recognized as a *TIME Magazine* Person of the Year for her work on the front lines of Ebola. She has hung out with Bono, spoken on a panel with Bill Gates, and been proposed to, jokingly, by Warren Buffet.

In her magnetizing raspy voice, Katie told me, "I've had to do so many things to keep this organization running. Actually when it all started, I funded my movement by donating my eggs to a fertility clinic, but every time I think about those girls and what their prospects are without me, I keep going. There's just not someone else there who's stepping up to do this for them, this is my mission on the planet, and so, if it comes out that I have to earn a million dollars a month to take care of these girls, I'm going to figure out how to do it, because what's the alternative?"

That's what I want you to feel like about your people: what's the alternative? Feel this first, and the money you need to fund your movement will come. But if you think, well, if the money comes, then I will go all in and love my people like Katie loves those little girls in Liberia, I'm sorry to say it's not going to work.

Katie wasn't ever going to end up bagging groceries in Bernardsville, New Jersey. Steve Jobs couldn't have ended up in some back-office coding job in Silicon Valley. His thoughts wouldn't have created that. Martin Luther King, Jr. was never going to run a nice, friendly local congregation in Alabama. Jesus was not going to end up with a quirky little carpentry biz.

When I say those things, it's preposterous, right? That's how I want you to feel. Who the hell else would do this?

What would happen to these people without me? You Feel This First. You feel this first and THEN the magic happens. It doesn't work the other way around, even when we want it to.

KEEPING IT SIMPLE

One you have your number and the desire, the next goal is to simplify the workload in order to make that amount of revenue. The reason I want you to do the least amount of work possible is, this movement is only going to grow with you. If we have a really complicated business, with lots of legs of the stool and lots of different things that you sell at lots of different price points and tons of ways that people can either donate or pay, and if it's really complicated, that's a business that can't grow with you, and that's a movement that's going to be hard to get people enlisted into.

Right now, as we're starting a movement, what we really need are what I'm calling your twelve apostles. Those are your early evangelists. Maybe it's your first hundred customers, even. Those are the clients who are going to provide the measure that shows this movement is moving, and when we get to that monthly dollar you're looking for, then we're going to re-evaluate this movement and see: is it time to hire people, is it time to broaden the primary pain point?

We are architecting your book to help us find the lowest hanging fruit possible as quickly as possible. Those are your most likely apostles. When you're hitting your number with those evangelists, with those apostles, then we might add on the next problem that they want to move away from. But what a lot of people try and do is, they try and add all the problems at once, and they try and sell the big solution. This is the equivalent of trying to sell an iPhone 6 Plus back in 2007 the year the iPhone was first released. If you are trying to sell yourself as the leader of a movement that's five years in the future, you miss out on the revenue that's waiting for you by being where you are right now.

MEASURABLE MILESTONES

I'm going to give you examples of what is and isn't a milestone.

Actual Milestone: five clients booked in the month of April at $1500 each

Not a Milestone: get more clients by launching a new website, doing a telesummit, going to start guest blogging

A milestone needs to be a binary question. So, "more clients" is not it. Speaking engagements? Probably can't measure the effectiveness of that. How will you know when to quit, when to change, when to keep going?

Our next milestone is not a 100,000 people around the world buying your T-shirts and taking pictures of themselves in it. An immediate milestone is something that you can imagine achieving within the next six months, something that's possible, and if you're having trouble identifying this, what you want to think about is small numbers—in most cases, smaller than what you're thinking.

And small numbers are what you want anyway. I worked with a group of women entrepreneurs who had a really well-designed, environmentally friendly product. Through a bit of luck and the fact that they had a great product, they made it on Oprah's Favorite Things list just months out of the gate. They rode the coat tails of that experience for over five years, and in that time they were fulfilling millions of dollars in orders, losing money, and descending into chaos. They had not built a movement (even though they desperately wanted to) and the early success actually distracted them, ultimately preventing them from making the difference they intended to make. Starting small is achievable, attainable, and manageable. We can grow with it and fund your movement in a way that leads to permanent change and meaningful legacy.

THE TOP OF THE FUNNEL

At the very top of your funnel, we have to create awareness about you and your movement in order to find those 12 apostles. Creating awareness can be very overwhelming because it's an endless list of possibilities. To start, I want you to limit the way people find out about you to one to three activities that we can measure if they're working, and turn them off or turn them up. The types of awareness activities at the top of the funnel could be Facebook ads or it could be Facebook posts, it could be LinkedIn, it could be Pinterest, it could be Google AdWords, it could be search engine optimization, it could be creating your own podcast, appearing on other people's podcasts, it could be speaking at events for free, it could be hosting meet-up groups.

I want you to pick one to three things that you're going to do and you're going to get really good at, and not give up on any of them for at least 90 days unless you get clear evidence that you should stop. You must master one channel before you move to the next channel. And this is really channel marketing. The one channel you pick should be the one thing that, right now, you are most connected to and feel the most delicious about.

FIRST ATTRACTION

The next level is a lead magnet. People will learn about you through those awareness channels. When they do, we want to send them somewhere—and that somewhere is your lead magnet. This is where people are going to pay you with their attention. That means they will exchange their email address and their time. Maybe it's their time reading a checklist, maybe it's their time taking a thirty-minute free class that you have, maybe it's their time watching a five-minute free video that you send them, but they're going to pay you in their attention. Your job, at this stage, now that you've got people's attention, is to get their email address. You can have a maximum of three lead magnets to start, but I recommend starting with one so you can figure out if it's working before introducing complications to your funnel.

Here are 20 ideas for lead magnets. Pick one and be frigging awesome at that one!

1. eCourse
2. Toolkit

3. Chapter of A Book

4. Video or Video Series

5. Guide, Special Report, or ebook Download

6. Software or Plugin

7. Audio Interview

8. Daily or Weekly Tips

9. Limited Time Offer or Free Shipping

10. Webinar or Teleseminar

11. How-to Audio Training

12. Free Private Facebook Group

13. A Half-Hour Consultation with You

14. A Coupon

15. Free Tickets to a Special Event

16. Free Samples

17. Contest or Sweepstakes

18. "Swipe File" (collection of templates that people can tailor to their own use)

19. Cheat Sheet/Handout

20. Quiz/Survey

a Leigh runs a lifestyle business called
fe. She is amazing, but when I spend
ya, what I do—totally true—is, I buy
is wearing. I buy her perfume, I buy her
hose, I buy er purse, I buy her sunglasses. She has this
effect on people. One of the things I said to Tonya,
that I would love from her as a lead magnet, is for her
to put out, every month, her favorite new products of
the month. What's the new perfume she bought, what
are the new earrings she's wearing?

Her Fascination Advantage, for those of you who
know Sally Hogshead's book *How to Fascinate*, is The
Connoisseur. As readers of Hogshead book know, The
Connoisseur is one of 49 personality archetypes and
your archetype helps you determine what makes you
most fascinating, and most valuable to the people
around you. When you match the lead magnet to your
fascination advantage, you'll have more fun creating
and sharing it and consumers will love it. That's why
a Buyer's Guide would be a perfect lead magnet for
Tonya. Now, my fascination advantage is The Victor,
and that's all about results, and so my lead magnet
needs to create results in advance for my prospect,

because they are not going to buy my beautiful taste in pantyhose or book covers. They're going to buy the results I get for my clients.

PUTTING OUT THE RIGHT OFFERS

I'm going to tell you, you can have one to three offers, but it's not going to surprise you to learn that I recommend starting with one. Get so good at that one offer that you could have other people selling it, you could deliver it in your sleep, you could write a book on it in three days and not blink twice, because you know it so well. You're going to be able to take parts of yourself and replicate yourself through video or audio recording.

Nail one offer for you that matches with your awareness strategy and with your lead magnet strategy. So, that one offer, what does that have to be? Remember that the way you want your reader to be different at the end of the book is that you want them to know X is possible for them, and you want them to know that it will be faster if they do it with you. So, that is your entry-level program, that's the first program you're going to complete. Even though everyone who joins this program won't have read your book, they still all want that outcome. They know they can do it on their own, but there's going to be a certain element of trial and error, and rather than the trial and error what they just want is to do it with you, get it right the first time, and nail that outcome.

My recommendation is that you make this no longer than three months, even just six to eight weeks, because you want them to see results from solving that problem as quickly and reasonably as you can. So now, voilá, you have a program!

How do you price it? Let's take that monthly number you got to and divide it by the number of clients you can handle. For most people, this is no more than 20 clients a month, and 10 is a little more realistic. If your number for each month was $10,000 and you are comfortable taking 10 clients, the price for your product is $1,000.

Now you have to message your program so it's clear why it's worth $1,000. For the people who really do everything, who really dive in, they should be able to get a 10X return on their investment. If I asked you to give me a ten dollar bill and I'll give you a hundred dollar bill back, would you say yes? I hope so! Everybody would say "yes" to that. That's what you should feel like about your program.

For some people who are selling something business related, this is a really easy one, because they can say, "Here's how much you're going to make when you do this and when you follow the plan." But if you're doing something like baby sleep coaching, or if you're doing something like helping moms prioritize their time, or helping people clarify their creative vision, you're going to have to get really clear in your head about what 10X the value of this program would be. Why would it be worth it, to your early adopter, to invest? How are they going to be ten times better off if they do this?

We're going to sell this to people either through a sales page or through a powerful sales conversation, and then we have one product we're selling and we have a limited number of slots, and we have a price point that's going to fund our movement. We're doing that because we are committed to this mission, not because we want to pay our bills. Just that shift in your thinking and your mindset is a big part of why people would buy from you.

THE INCUBATED AUTHOR

If a part of you is thinking, "I need to do this because I need to pay my mortgage this month," it will come through in the spaces in between the letters you type on the keyboard. I do not think this is magical, but I think it works in a way that feels like magic. When your energy changes to an energy of true service, you leave that graspy, "I need to do this or I'm going to have to get a full-time job" space. People are more attracted to working with you, and I think what happens is that you literally write completely different emails without realizing it.

When you can create that picture for them, of what that vision is, and it's not about you but it's really about them, that is when the energy shifts and the mindset shifts.

If you work this simple formula, without excuses or arguments—almost like a scientist—for 90 days straight, you will have a lot of information about what is working and what isn't. You will be steering by facts and not just your gut. The goal behind all of this is to create a tipping point for you. So, you want to reach a point where the growth of your movement is inevitable, and it's kind of like rolling a snowball down a long hill of fresh snow. You will know when you are hitting this point when you get magnitudes more output than what you're personally putting into it, and that's when you're getting referrals, and when you're getting people wearing your T-shirts and posting about it. You don't start with that because of a great T-shirt design, because no one will see the T-shirt! And that, I think, is one of the big myths that I really want you to see. It's so much more effective to start with getting these metaphorical twelve apostles, then get them out there talking about you, as a way to reach the tipping point.

In the short term, what that might look like and feel like is, "Oh, my vision got so much smaller," but what I want you to see is that the five-year plan feeds into that bigger vision. Right now, today, the way you feed that bigger vision is that you serve these people now, the ones in front of you now, with all your heart and soul and everything you have. That will give us the evidence that we need to keep going, so you don't have to keep switching your movement, switching your ideas, changing how you employ your tactics.

When I talk about The Incubated Author, what we're incubating is that big vision, and the way we're getting there is with these little, measurable steps.

INSIDE THE AUTHOR INCUBATOR
On Picking What's Right for You

Q: I did *The Fascination Advantage* and I'm "The Intrigue." My primary advantage is passion, second is mystique, and dormant is alert, but I still did not figure out what my lead magnet should be, based on that. How would you figure it out?

A: I really could see you doing the videos that you're not even in but you're maybe doing the voiceover of, really creating mystery around it, and excitement about what it can be. A great thing for you to do is create a video trailer for your movement, one that is totally exciting, but doesn't give anything away.

I also wonder if you could do a "Create Your Own Vision Board" Kit and give out printable images that people could put on their vision board. You could even say, "Hey, we're all going to hold space to make this vision a reality, and the way we're going to do that is that you're going to post a picture of your vision board in the group." The kit could include this download that you'll get from me, plus membership in my group, because that's how we're going to make your vision board more of a reality." So now, they're in your Facebook group, and you have their email address.

There's one other thing you can do. It's a little weird, but it does work. I actually learned it from Jack Canfield. Take a few lead magnet ideas and put the name of each on a note card. Then have a friend help you by holding up one card at a time while you say the sentence, "The perfect lead magnet for me right now is the 'Vision Board Toolkit.'" As you are saying this sentence, extend one arm out to the side and keep it straight. Have your friend press down on this arm. If the lead magnet is a fit, you'll be able to resist the downward pressure and hold your arm rigid. If not, you won't.

Even though this is totally different than the Fascination Advantage, many people get the same result. Maybe your subconscious mind delivers the right answer for you. My lead magnet ideas could be the world's best suggestions, but if it doesn't feel good to you, it won't work anyway, so don't do it, because that's just no fun.

CHAPTER SIX

GOING ALL IN ON SERVING YOUR GREATER PURPOSE

"THE DIFFERENCE IN WINNING AND LOSING IS MOST OFTEN... NOT QUITTING."

WALT DISNEY

Since 1994, I have helped hundreds of people get their books written, published, and promoted. Some of these authors have successfully built strong movements. And some haven't. The determining factor was rarely tactics or resources. The determining factor is one small decision. It's a decision I can't teach you how to make and I can't make it for you. And it's a decision you may not even know you have made until you are successful. Motivational speaker Les Brown says, "It's not over until you win." Nelson Mandela said, "It always seems impossible until it's done." Those are the mindsets winners have.

Many of the authors I work with told me for months that what they were trying to do felt impossible. And then they did it and they wanted more. When you know how strong you are and what you are capable of, your dreams will only get bigger.

The first time I hired a personal trainer, I thought the work-outs would kill me. The first week of racing around the aerobics room head down, pushing a square of carpet, or jumping onto boxes 24 inches off the ground, or, God help me, doing those fucking endless squats that I could never get the position right on.

I couldn't wait for week two or week 22 when things would get EASIER.

Finally, somewhere around week 12, I couldn't resist. I breezily asked my trainer, mid-lunge, "So, Bryan, when is this going to get easier?"

He looked at me, puzzled. Truly stumped. It was as if I'd asked a question in Amharic.

"Easier? Why would it get easier?"

"You know, when I'm thinner and stronger and good at all this stuff."

He laughed. "Oh, as you get thinner and stronger, we just make the work-outs more intense. It will always be this hard!"

GO ALL IN

The question before you now that you have seen laid out what starting a movement looks like and what it really requires of you is:

Are you ready to go all in?

Most people ride the clutch and mash the gas at the same time. They are half in and half out.

Riding the clutch means that the clutch is partly engaged, by pressing the pedal in part way. The clutch is used to engage the engine with the transmission, not to speed up or slow down the car. That is what the gas pedal and brake pedal are for. When you do this, the clutch becomes warped and eventually fails.

When you do this with your movement, you will never truly know what was possible. Your results will be warped and your efforts will fail. You might try to blame the car for being a lemon or the movement for being a bad idea, but really, you didn't give it a fair chance.

If instead of wanting a movement, you wanted a 9–5 job and you accepted an offer, you wouldn't be thinking, "Eh, maybe it will work out, maybe it won't." If you started a college degree you wouldn't think, "Eh, what's $50k a year, if it doesn't work out, I'll quit." But somehow in business we have made it okay, honorable even, to have a back-up plan at the ready. I'm saying, take it off the table.

If you are all in for this New Bliss that you are moving towards, then it really requires, at the fundamental level, a commitment to overcoming approximately a million obstacles. It's not like you just decide, and then, oh, now magically everything's easy. No, almost the opposite: that's when the challenges really start to heat up.

Maybe you remember the story of Adam Walsh, a boy who was abducted in Florida in 1981. His parents, most notably, his father, John Walsh, immediately started a movement when their son was missing. From the ad hoc organization they put together to help with the search for Adam, they established the Adam Walsh Child Resource Center, which eventually merged with the National Center for Missing & Exploited Children (NCMEC), which they co-founded in 1984.

I know this is scary and unpleasant to think about, but imagine the commitment you would have to your movement if your movement was dedicated to the search for your missing child? There would be no hint of riding the clutch. You wouldn't fall for the delusional thought that things should be easy, and you wouldn't look at an obstacle that came up in that process of trying to save him and say, "Well, you know what? I'm not that into my son anyway, I guess I'll just quit looking and get a corporate job."

There ARE, for *sure* going to be challenges that come up. There are going to be many times where you need to pivot, and many difficult decisions that you need to make. There are going to be times where it seems like it's not worth it. But all of that self-doubt, all of those issues that come up, if it was a matter of saving your child, you would keep doing it.

People come to me all the time with the idea for their book. They're imagining being on the Oprah couch, and to get there, or to your Ted Talk, or your New York Times bestseller list, you need to have a commitment to a movement that is much bigger than a business revenue goal. A lot of people don't do the work to identify their movement, and so they're only kind of committed to something that's only kind of clarified. And then they want a magical angel to sprinkle pixie dust on them in exchange for almost having a fully-formed idea.

Despite these fantasies, I think what we really want is to build and grow and develop something where that money naturally follows as evidence that we're doing something meaningful. I think, for most of you, that if you would just wake up with money in your bank account but with a stipulation that the only way you could collect that money is if you were committed to never helping anyone again, you would walk away from that bounty. There is no price worth a guaranteed knowing that we didn't make a difference.

That's why the first and most important metric is being truly committed to funding your movement. When you do that, you show up for your movement in a bigger way than your movement might feel right now. The reason you are going to be willing to do this work, even though this is really hard work, is your belief in the New Bliss you are driving toward and the awareness that the only way to get to this New Bliss that we want to get people to, is to get our apostles.

CREATE SERVICES AND PRODUCTS FOR THE PURPOSE OF SELLING THEM.

Your logo doesn't matter, your company name doesn't matter, your website doesn't matter. These are ego things you GET to do, but they are not what will determine your success. The first step is to make something sellable and sell it. Here's how master marketing expert Dan Kennedy describes it: "Years ago, I discovered the #1 thing I should focus on in business: making saleable things and selling them. And I can't tell you how happy I am to have had that revelation early in life. Without it, I most certainly would have struggled to survive, let alone grow my business. Because one of the biggest problems that stops businesses from growing and also gets businesses quickly into trouble is failing to focus on making sales."

This is true for movements as well. That doesn't mean you have to build out the whole product to sell it, you just need to build the marketing. Most people are going to invest in most products for the results, not the aesthetics. (I mean, unless you are building the next Apple!) So what you need in order to make offers is to have the marketing and the sales mechanisms in place. You can create the actual product after they buy.

I actually did that in order to write this book. I knew I wanted to write about Starting a Movement and that I had a big list of findings to share, but it wasn't fully fleshed out. So I created a live three-day event called Start a Movement and a virtual six-week course with the same name. I sold these events based on some Facebook posts and phone calls. I knew the RESULT of the training would be a solid understanding of what it takes to change an industry or a group of people. What I promised these early buyers is that they would know how to start a movement of their own and that they would know the exact steps they would need to take to get there. I generated over $100,000 from this offer and yet, I hadn't written this book yet. There was no website for this program, no student center, no videos had been created, no worksheets designed, no audio trainings completed in order to collect that revenue. The first dollars rolled in about four weeks before I had to start teaching the material and so it was at that point, after I made that first six figures, that I began to create the worksheets, PowerPoints, and call scripts. Even now, as I am writing this, my amazing video guy, Max Fox, is sending over the videos we made at the live event, and John and Robin on my team are uploading them to our new student center. (They will be ready when you are, dear reader. Email me at Angela@TheAuthorIncubator.com for details! Still no website yet!)

This is my point. Make something sellable and sell it. If it doesn't sell, for the love of God, don't write a book that no one will read or create a website no one will ever go to!

If you don't have a Primary Pain Point that inspires those early adopters to buy, then that is the data that you need to go and create something sellable. What you have learned from the marketplace, because marketing always works even though we don't always like what it tells us, is that if you can't sell it now, you're not going to be able to sell it after you make it.

You have to be able to sell at least a few copies on your own, *mano a mano*, before you go and scale something, build it out, or otherwise decide that it's not working. I see a lot of people quitting before they've even gotten the feedback on a product that will work.

Even if you've pick the "wrong" thing, if you go all in it will become the thing you needed to get you to the "right" thing. Let's say you really think your movement is backyard chicken farms. Iif you go all in on backyard chicken farms with no hesitation, you're going to find out so much sooner what you're really here for. If you go half in, it will take you twice as long to learn that your real calling is feng shui. Having the clarity behind the Chicken Movement sends a signal to the Universe that you are available for transmission. When you are all over the place with ideas, the Universe doesn't know how to get a clear message through. Going all in on something creates the space for the right things to show up for you.

WHEN YOU FIND SOMETHING THAT WORKS, STICK WITH IT

Once you find something that works, stop changing course. Changing course is for people who don't want to make a difference. If you have created something and sold it, it works. The Universe wants you to do MORE of that. Grow it. Nurture it. Do it better.

As soon as you see something work, you may get a rush of confidence that will make you think, "You know, it would be awesome right now to sell an ABC widget." No! Unless you have the extra bandwidth to do that, that's not a choice you should make. My advice is to first make sure you're selling out of your XYZ widget and you're comfortably hitting your funding goals.

Once that's going, and it's smooth sailing and you have some extra time, then if you want to add the ABC widget, okay. But being bored or even being inspired are not excuses to abandon your followers.

Think about MLK, or your Jesus or whoever started the movement that inspires you and your work, and think about them saying to you, "Look, I was going to keep this whole Civil Rights movement going, but I thought about it and I realized this whole abortion debate is heating up and there are starving children in Africa so I'm going to go work on those issues, but don't go anywhere, I'll probably come back to this whole equal under the law concept soon!" Would you admire that? Would that have turned out to be the person who you most look up to? Nope! That person's flaky and you probably wouldn't even notice them. They probably wouldn't even make your radar, that's the thing.

This level of focus, this is service, devotion, prayer.

You will be tempted to "cheat" on your movement. And each decision you make to resist or overcome those temptations will attract more people to your movement. You will get stronger and stronger in your commitment to serve the people this movement was designed for. This life is almost monastic, and that's how I want you to feel about your work.

When you change your mind, you're sending a signal to the Universe that you don't want success, and your wish will be granted. When you nurture and show gratitude for something that's working, you'll get more of it.

OKAY SQUARESPACE, WE'LL BUILD IT BEAUTIFUL...BUT LATER

Most people start their movement with a logo and a website, but often not anything to sell. They're not things people resonate with, they are usually the New Bliss that we're moving towards, and not enough of the Primary Pain Point we're moving away from. Once you find the thing that's selling and can fund your movement, then do the branding. When you hit your monthly revenue goals, take some of that money and invest in an amazing branding person who could give you not just a logo that you're proud of, but a whole style guide that blows you away and really speaks to the exact evangelists you're looking for. Here's where I would get the trademarks, make your website beautiful, make sure you get a style document that really speaks to your movement, maybe build a program website.

I want you to be able to hit that monthly revenue goal in the least amount of time possible so that we can get you on the next stage, so we can get you either in media or PR or speaking. How can we take this movement further up that innovation chain, from just the early adopters to starting to reach that tipping point?

You don't want to do this until you have a lot of support behind you. You want to have case studies, you want to have your program, you want to have all your intellectual property locked down. You want to know you have something unique.

CONSTRAIN YOUR FOCUS.

Now stop testing offers and constrain your focus. Start to say no 10 times more than you say yes. Until you meet your monthly goals, don't take on anything new. Constraining your focus is the greatest way you can show that you love your movement and the people your movement is for.

You want to know you have something that works, and then you're going to constrain your focus so that you can hit that same goal in less time. What was taking you ten hours a day, I'd love to see taking you two hours a day before you move onto the next thing. That means you're going to outsource, you're going to start to scale your business so other people can do aspects of it, because there is only one you and your movement needs you for bigger and better things now.

Build the support team, the infrastructure, the processes you neXed to start to become more removed from your day-to-day operations.

INVEST IN YOURSELF

Are you an awesome bet? If you were placing odds on who was going to win, would you bet on yourself? If not, fix that now. Be an awesome bet! My authors tell me, "Without you, my book wouldn't have happened," and it's true. I get results for my clients—but THEY do the work. They show up and step into the space I hold for them.

When you decide you're going to make an investment in your movement, you need to know that the best possible bet you could place is on yourself. When you invest in yourself, and when you know you're going to have your own back, you serve the whole system at a higher level. The people who show up for you will be able to do a better job and you will be able to receive what they are giving by creating an environment for them to really be able to help you.

You have the opportunity to get better returns than any stock on the open market would ever get. A great stock might get a 10 percent return. You should be able to make a $10,000 investment in yourself and know you're going to get not only more than a 10 percent return, you should know that you're going to get a 100% return. So instead of investing $10,000 and making $1,000 (which would be a great experience with a stock), I want you to invest $10,000 in yourself and get $100,000 back.

When you believe in yourself, you will always get better returns than any stock on the open market.

MANAGE YOUR DRAMA

The hardest part of running a business is managing the drama your business is designed to create in your head. The drama is coming. Do you have a plan to address it?

I'll use my Jesus example here. Jesus said, "I have come into the world as light, so that whoever believes in me may not remain in darkness. If anyone hears my words and does not keep them, I do not judge him; for I did not come to judge the world but to save the world." (It's not the best marketing copy, but we'll go with it for the moment.) When your mission is that big, you know there's going to be drama! Martin Luther King, Jr. was assassinated. Jesus was martyred.

This is your calling. The drama is a collection of little angel messengers that are not to be wished away. Those are all the lessons that you need to learn to do this work at the next level. That's the Universe testing you and saying, "Are you up for this? Are you open to this? You said you wanted it, did you mean it? Do you know what that's going to require?" It's all there to prepare you.

There is actually nothing external that qualifies you to be the leader of your movement. There is no degree or certification or life experience or anything that you can do, externally, that would make you qualified to run your movement. The thing that makes you qualified to run your movement is your ability to manage the increasing and intensifying drama that running this particular movement requires.

Now, it does get easier to manage, because I will tell you that the key to managing drama is practicing. Knowing that you can handle it is one of the most valuable lessons that you can learn in leadership. When you decide to stop—stop sabotaging your movement because you're not sure if you're big enough for it—that's when you're big enough for it.

As your business grows, the drama gets more intense, not less! There is no date in the future coming when you have this all figured out and it's easy.

Know the drama's coming and have a plan to address it. Relish the drama and the intensity, because it means you are worthy of these lessons. Enjoy the opportunity to manage the drama and you'll get more, bigger drama to manage. You deserve it! You have been anointed as a steward of the Universe's money, a steward of the Universe's wishes to make the planet better, and as you prove yourself worthy to hold that space, you will get more and more sent to you.

INSIDE THE AUTHOR INCUBATOR
On How Much to Give Away

Q: When it comes to really testing the market, how do I give away the why but not the how?

A: What a lot of people will do for their free calls is they'll break down a problem, and then they give you the actual answers to that problem. I used to do this on my calls all the time. So, I would have a free call titled "How to Write a Great Title for Your Book," and then I would go give people a lot of homework. I'd tell them to go find ten titles and make a list of every possible title and then create some Facebook posts and go on Facebook and post the titles and see which one gets the most clicks, then pick the three that got the most clicks and then test the top three with Facebook ads.

I was giving them so much homework that the feedback I'd get was, "I'm going to do all the stuff you gave me to do for free, and then I'm going to come back and work with you, because I love you, I think you're brilliant, I totally want to work with you, I just want to get this title done now, and I feel like you've given me a ton of really good ideas. I'm going to put them into action."

But of course they would go away and get busy, or overwhelmed with my instructions, and they would never get that title so they felt embarrassed to call me, or I just went on some never-to-be-looked-at-again to-do list. It didn't work. I didn't REALLY help them, even though that was my stated goal.

So now, I don't give them that level of specificity and I don't give them that homework.

I will just tell them stories and I will give them examples and the opportunity to talk to me about their situation on a private call.

Let's say you wanted to teach about boundaries. You might give examples of what happens when you don't set boundaries. Or examples of what happens when you set a healthy boundary. But I wouldn't necessarily tell them, "For you, here is what I want you to do, create one small rule, go put that rule into action, see what happens, when you get a response, journal about it, then I want you to write a letter to your future self that says what you're going to do when somebody pushes the boundary." That's the stuff you do with a client. Before they're a client, you're going to give them the examples and the stories.

You can't teach them everything about boundaries, give them a chance to go out and practice, and solve the problem. On a free call, all you can do is help them to see there is a gap between where they are and where they want to be, and that the key to closing that gap is working with you.

CHAPTER SEVEN

CLEAR EYES, FULL HEARTS, CAN'T LOSE.

"OBSTACLES ARE THOSE FRIGHTFUL THINGS YOU SEE WHEN YOU TAKE YOUR EYES OFF YOUR GOAL."

HENRY FORD

In the now-cancelled fictional football drama *Friday Night Lights*, (which, incidentally, was based on H.G. "Buzz" Bissinger's non-fiction book of the same name), Coach Taylor takes a high school team and turns it into a movement to unite a community. The night before the final playoffs, he gives a speech I hope you can replay for yourself in the moments you need it. He said:

"Right now, 40,000 people have also written us off. But there are some who do still believe in you, a few who'd never give up on you. When you take that field, those are the people I want in your minds. Those are the people I want in your hearts. Every man at some point is gonna lose a battle. He's gonna fight and he's gonna lose. But what makes him a man, is that in the midst of that battle he does not lose himself. This game is not over, this battle is not over. So let's hear it one more time, together. Clear eyes, full hearts, CAN'T LOSE!"

THERE ARE ALTERNATIVES, BUT NOT EASY ONES

This is going to be hard. You are absolutely, for sure, without a doubt, going to want to quit. In fact as I am typing this chapter, not one, not two, but *three* of the members of my mentorship just sent me a "request to quit" notice. Most people will agree it's the right thing to do. You don't have to work so hard; pick up a nice part time job at a flower shop. I hear driving for Uber is a great way to make cash and meet people!

If you can look at a picture of your first apostle and think, "She'd be fine without me," then maybe quitting is for you.

Although let's be clear about one thing first: starting a business without a movement behind it is ONLY harder and filled with more obstacles. Unless you have a big trust fund, you need to run a business to fund your movement. Running a business is hard. That's why most people, instead of running a business, have a hobby that isn't particularly financially successful but they call it a business because it sounds nicer at a cocktail parties.

Having a reason for running your business like a business actually makes things easier. You have your 'why' to keep you buoyed up in the dark moments. But if you can't make the business work with a movement, let's be super clear this significantly decreases your chances of success without a movement.

So what are the things that will increase your success?

First and foremost is loving your people with your heart, mind, and soul.

WITHOUT ACCOUNTABILITY YOU WILL ABANDON YOUR PEOPLE

One way to show that love is to make a sacrifice on their behalf to keep you accountable. This can be a mentor, a coach, or even an employee. But there needs to be someone outside of you who's holding you accountable to the promises you made to your movement.

When I started my business, I gave myself an offer letter. I wrote a job description, gave myself a board of directors (my roommate, my sister, and two good friends), and I had a monthly call with them where I had to tell them what I did the last month and what I was going to do the next month. And let me tell you, they asked some really hard questions! I caught myself several times lying to them or leaving information out because I didn't want to explain what I was doing, but really those were ways I wasn't serving my movement. Month one, I said my goal was twenty-four clients for an online $100 class I was teaching. I thought it would be easy! It was only $100. I got one. One lone client. I wanted to lie. I hoped they didn't remember. They did. And they wanted the plan for how we were going to make up for it next month. And they wanted to know next time how we could address it earlier in the month. They explained that there was a point when I realized I wasn't going to hit that goal and that's when they wished I called so we could put a plan in place before the month was over. Having a board made me smarter and braver.

You can even turn your business success into a game. At the beginning of the month or the quarter, create rewards for hitting certain goals. Create penalties for not hitting those goals. With your rewards, you want to be careful that you don't reward yourself with something you would buy anyway. For instance, don't make it a haircut, because you probably get your hair cut anyway, but if you normally go to a $45 haircut place, but there's a place that you would love to get your haircut that's a $150, make it that place.

If you have a mushy outcome in mind—something like, "I want as many clients as possible," or "I want to make more money than last month," you're going to do a whole bunch of things to try to make that happen, and you're going to get varied results that you don't know how to interpret. But if you're trying to get one outcome, let's say, ten clients at a $1000 each, then your brain is going to get assigned the task of figuring out how to get you there. Having one goal makes you exponentially smarter and more capable of tapping into your own intelligence.

YOU FIRST. BUT ONLY EVERY TIME.

I'm going to give you a secret bonus tip. I hesitate to do this because you won't believe me now, and by the time you get this lesson for yourself, you will have long forgotten I said it to you. But for the one or two of you who are at the edge of a breakthrough, this little bit of information will put you over the edge.

Back in Step Eight in Chapter 3, I wrote a lot about how you wanted to bring your early adopters into the hero's story and make it their story, too—especially in the ordinary world. Well, the truth is that it IS their story, too. The illusion that we are separate beings is just that, an illusion. Philosopher Alan Watts argues, "We do not 'come into' this world; we come out of it, as leaves from a tree. As the ocean 'waves' the universe 'peoples.' Every individual is an expression of the whole realm of nature, a unique action of the total universe. This fact is rarely, if ever, experienced by most individuals. Even those who know it to be true in theory do not sense or feel it, but continue to be aware of themselves as isolated 'egos' inside bags of skin."

Your desire to make the pain in your life mean something or to be able to make a difference, comes from, I believe, "the myth of the sole ego."

Everything that happens in your Movement is happening both TO you and FOR you. There is no separation. The way you buy from others will be the way others buy from you. The way you treat your clients or employees will be the way your clients and employees treat you. Philosophers Gilles Deleuze and Félix Guattari call this the rhizome.

"As a model for culture, the rhizome is characterized as a map or wide array of attractions and influences with no specific origin or genesis, for a 'rhizome has no beginning or end; it is always in the middle, between things, interbeing, intermezzo.' The rhizome resists chronology and organization, instead favoring a nomadic system of growth and propagation. Culture spreads like the surface of a body of water, spreading towards available spaces or trickling downwards towards new spaces through fissures and gaps, eroding what is in its way."

I know I'm not supposed to bring my PhD in Post Modern Philosophy out to play too much but if any of this is sounding like coming home to you, what you have to know is that you have the opportunity to fix this. You will always be one tiny step ahead of your followers. If people start missing payments, see what payments you are missing. If people are complaining about your leadership, see whose leadership you are complaining about. The "You First" approach works—but only every time, as author Byron Katie might say.

BECOMING THE LEADER YOU
ARE REQUIRED TO BE

If there was a single quote that's had the biggest impact on the way I spend my money, build my career, and live my life, it's this one by Jim Rohn: "You are the average of the five people you spend the most time with." Although I'll be honest, I don't know Jim Rohn and always thought it was Tim Ferriss who said it! Shows you who I'm hanging out with.

This concept is different than it might appear on paper, so let me explain. When I first started working on books, I worked with authors who were paid six-figure advances and had long, illustrious writing careers. None of the authors I worked for wrote books that didn't get published. They didn't write on spec. They had a contract and a deadline and a system for getting the book done by that deadline, and I was a part of the process. It's possible I could have gotten a job for some other type of writer who didn't finish his work—or ship his work, as author Seth Godin might say.

Because of these early experiences, I just became someone who regularly wrote and finished books.

When I did this inside corporate America, I was working for people who used books to sell products. We didn't sometimes just do a book because we had a fun idea, there was a discipline to our thinking and metrics that we had to meet for me to keep my job.

But when I started working with life coaches on their books, something changed. I started hanging out with people (amazing, wonderful, lovely people) who wanted to WANT to write books. They didn't know that, of course, they thought they wanted a book, but they didn't have books. They actively liked the idea of having one, but not enough to really do anything about it.

I had clients who didn't finish their books. I had several book projects that were going unfinished. I had 10 or 20 people each week joining programs of mine and then never finishing their books. I was surrounded by and living in OPEN LOOPS. One day—after reading this quote from Tim Ferriss (☺)—I realized I had to change who I was spending time with.

If I started to spend time with people whose lives were filled with closed loops, probably, organically, the open loops in my life would begin to close.

Now that's not to say for a minute that I stopped loving my life coach friends and their open loops. I love them. But I choose not to spend as much time with them. I invite them to be a part of my new world, but here I only hold space for people who are ready to risk their fragile egos in service to the world. It's scary out here. But it's also brave and free.

I did Danielle LaPorte's *Desire Map* process a couple years back and the core desired feelings that came to me were fearless, grounded, and open-armed. In her process, she teaches you to pursue those feelings rather than specific goals. In the process of pursuing those feelings, I have, organically, changed the five people I spend the most time with, and in the process dramatically changed the results I see in my own life.

I think of this process as becoming NOW—in advance of the results you seek—the person you need to be to get the results you want.

So ask yourself, what kind of mentor would the person running your movement at, say, $1MM year in revenue and 10,000 fans and followers, invest in? Who would that person hang out with? How much would that person weigh? How often would that person get her eyebrows waxed? What brand of coffee would that person buy? Who would the last three texts on that person's phone be from?

When you get to know, love, and be the leader of the movement you want to build, your movement will be sitting under your nose.

CONCLUSION

I'm going to make a guess that at this point in our relationship, you have read the book, thought the ideas were great, but you still don't think you have an idea that's "good enough" to be the basis of a movement.

I'm going to guess that you are like Caroline Greene, best-selling author of the book *Matter* who has helped dozens of moms find work and start businesses that are right for them and their families and who still, even after making a difference changing so many people's lives, wonders if her message is worthy of a movement.

I bet you are like Sophie Sabbage, best-selling author of *The Cancer Whisperer*, who still worries she will be pigeon-holed as a cancer expert and never reach the broader audience she wants to help, even though people without cancer have signed up to work with her since her book was released.

I bet you are like Melissa Nations, whose revolutionary book *Skinny* has a powerful message for young girls who want to be thin, that that dream is possible without the self-harm and the shame that comes with it, who wonders if there is enough of her to go around and if it's fair to put her book out there without the ability to make a full-time commitment to her movement.

You could get lost right here in this quest to get every aspect of your movement perfect before you start. You could go straight back to "trying" to figure it out. But you know who that helps? No one.

Kevin Nations told me a story once that has stuck with me. I was telling him that I realized my authors needed more support after their books were released, but that I was having trouble figuring out what to offer or how to offer it. "Trying to figure it out doesn't exist," he said. "You are either helping your authors, or you're not. And you are basically telling them you don't care what happens to them."

"I do care," I protested.

"Imagine I was on a boat with your 8-year-old son," Kevin offered. "And let's say he didn't know how to swim, didn't have a life jacket on, and he fell off the back of that boat. Now there are two possibilities: either I jump in and save your kid, or I don't. If I stood on the deck and tried to think of the safest way to save him, or if I figured it would be better to take off my pants before I jumped in, or if I went looking for a life jacket and in that time your child drowned, you know what we'd call it? Negligence! And that is what you are being with your authors."

I hung up the phone and created The Order of the Plume, my mentorship program for authors, right after that call. It wasn't perfect, or fully formulated, or done elegantly, but I did it because I loved my authors and I wasn't going to watch them drown and call it helping.

What I learned in the process is that you think you are looking for your movement, but the truth is, your movement is looking for you. As Elizabeth Gilbert so beautifully said in her book, *Big Magic,* "The universe buries strange jewels deep within us all, and then stands back to see if we can find them."

If you are called to help people, if you know you were meant for something bigger, if sugar plums dance in your dreams nightly with ideas for how you can make a bigger difference, then the time for waiting has passed. Each idea is an attempt from the universe to get you to rise and stand in your greatness. The movement will come to you when you show up, in full, to the party. And that is my wish for you: stop waiting and show up for your people, imperfectly, and let the light shine through.

As an incubator, our goal is to speed up the growth and success of the movement with an inspiring community, quality advice, and a supportive structure. Not everyone wants to be incubated. Some people like the challenge of doing it on their own, even if it takes longer. The Author Incubator puts primacy on speed. In this environment, there is a lot of potential for cross-pollination of ideas and possible alliances and synergies.

THE INCUBATED AUTHOR

- ☐ Knows they were born to make a difference.
- ☐ Fears not being of service MORE than not getting it right.
- ☐ Wants to live each day knowing the struggles they faced were not in vain and that if they can save one person from even a fraction of pain, they will.
- ☐ Values speed and thinks of themselves as someone with no time to lose.
- ☐ Invests in improvement as a pay-it-forward style gift to the movement

Don't let anyone tell you that you can't start a movement with your message. The right book can ignite an adventure that draws your people to you, and with the right strategy and support in place you can fund your movement and create a legacy of transforming people's lives with joy and ease.

Ask yourself: what is the gospel, what is the sermon that you need to give to move people away from their pain and to see the New Bliss? When you find that, you create a movement your first apostles have no choice but to be a part of. They will be called. And that, ladies and gentlemen, is how you start a movement with your message.

10 THINGS
WE BELIEVE AT
THE AUTHOR
INCUBATOR

1. Every author we publish must have a servant's heart
    and be dedicated to creating change for their READER.

2. It's best to do one thing really, really well.

3. Getting a book than can make a difference out as
    quickly as possible is always better than waiting for the
    perfect book.

4. Money is an energetic exchange that is REQUIRED
    to create change and the acquisition of money is evi-
    dence you are creating that change.

5. Our OBSESSION is with serving READERS not
    AUTHORS.... The reader knows best; if the author
    knew best, they would not be working with us.

6. Authors should be making lots of money from their books.

7. We deliver RESULTS for our authors. That means we set strong boundaries and hold ONLY a place for their success.

8. We deliver WOW through RESULTS.

9. Our advice is often counter-intuitive and not always comfortable.

10. The old publishing model where publishers take 90% of the revenue is DEAD. In the new model, there must be an even trade of value between publisher and author.

ABOUT THE
AUTHOR

Dr. Angela E. Lauria is the founder of The Author Incubator™ and creator of the Difference Process™ for writing a book that matters.

She has helped hundreds of coaches and entrepreneurs write, publish, and promote best-selling books and has published over 130 books including Susan Hyatt's *Create your Own Luck* and Elizabeth DiAlto's *UnTame Yourself.*

She is the author of *The Difference: 10 Essentials to Freeing Your Inner Author & Writing a Book that Matters* (Difference Press, 2014), *If I'm So Smart, Why Can't I Be Happy* (Difference Press, 2013), and *From Medea to Media: Live Performance as a Vehicle for Social Change* (Atropos Press, 2009); the co-editor of *The World Almanac of US Politics* (Pharos Books, 1997); and an editor and researcher for *NIGHTMOVER: The Aldrich Ames Story* (HarperCollins, 1995), *Hong Kong 1997 and Beyond* (Summit Publishing Group, 1996), and *Aboard Air Force One* (Fithian Press, 1997).

Her clients can be seen everywhere from O Magazine to MSNBC.com. Angela has a PhD in Communications from The European Graduate School (EGS) in Saas Fee, Switzerland and holds coaching certificates from Martha Beck International and The International Institute of Coaching Studies (IICS). She has spoken before audiences at many events including the International Coaching Federation annual event, Which Test Won? Marketing conference, Blog World, and Lean Start Up D.C. In 2011, the IICS named her their Empowerment Coach of the Year. She lives in The Author Castle in McLean, Virginia with her husband Paul, her son Jesse, and their ebony- and ivory-colored Castle cats.

THANK YOU!

Thanks for reading! I'd love to hear more about your message and the movement you'd like to start. Please email me or comment on Facebook at:

https://www.facebook.com/TheAuthorIncubator

FREE VIDEO CLASS

For a collection of Start a Movement video training highlights, email:

Angela@TheAuthorIncubator.com

FREE BOOK

You can buy a copy of my book *The Difference: 10 Steps to Writing a Book that Matters* over on Amazon, but I'm happy to stick a copy in the mail to you—totally free, autographed, and with a few other secret treats and surprises, too. Here's what you have to do to get it:

1. Schedule a Strategy Session with my team at www.TheAuthorIncubator.com/Apply

2. Show UP to the Strategy Session—No shows and cancellations will not be rewarded. This makes my team cranky.

3. On your call, let the editor know you'd like us to send you a free copy of the book.

When you get the book (and all the other surprises in the Movement-maker care package), be sure to drop a review on Amazon or post a picture of yourself holding the book on Facebook or Instagram!

ACKNOWLEDGEMENTS

This book idea came together over Kevin and Melissa Nations' kitchen table in Columbus, Ohio one steamy August day. Without that conversation and our partnership, I might have missed the opportunity to take my own work to the next level. I'm grateful to have them both in my life and my business.

From August to November, I got a little busy. I got married, hosted 4 events, and I moved into a Castle. I put the book on hold until a magical fairy princess walked through my Castle doors. Rachael Maddox, whose first book is publishing the same day as this one, came into my life in a whirlwind of activity on November 5th, 2015. Her surprise appearance at our Three Days to Done event and her deep commitment to her movement inspired me to stop hiding the light of this book. I knew this message was important and needed to be heard, but I was afraid I wasn't ready, afraid I didn't have time to get it right, afraid I didn't have enough to say yet. And then I met Rachael and I realized when we are called, we must do what seems impossible before we feel ready. I hope you'll buy her book, *Secret Bad Girl*. It seems odd for a client to inspire *me* to write a book, but she was the unexpected angel I needed to make the birth of this book happen. We meet our midwives in unexpected places and in surprising ways. I remain open to teachers in all forms and fashions—especially pretty curly-haired ones who play a mean ukulele and write some killer poetry.

To the folks who trusted me and signed up for the Start a Movement program before I had created it: Randi Rubenstein, Jodi Jenson-Schuelke, Michelle Richards, Amber McLean, Meka West, Steph Gold, Cassie Parks, Kimberlie Chenoweth, Jill Angie, Tami Stacklehouse, Kathleen Harper, and Andrea Hanson. Thank you for participating in the live and virtual events that form the foundational work of this book and the program. Your questions, feedback, and companionship made this journey possible. Each and every one of you has a movement I believe in and I am so honored to be a part of your journey to making it a reality. Stand in service to your people proudly. You have been chosen to lead.

The Author Incubator continues to grow and flourish. We are blessed with an incredible team and I am so grateful for their commitment to our mission to revolutionize the publishing industry. In no particular order, thanks go to TAI team members Mila Nedeljkov, Robin Thompson, John Matthews, Kelly Pratt, Grace Kerina, Flavia Belli, Heidi Miller, Kate Makled, Max Fox, Mark Butler, Melissa Nations, Lautaro Cabrera, Angela Clark, Alvin Ramirez, and my husband Paul Brycock who is also a critical member of the team—in more ways than most people will ever realize.

There are four special women who this book would not have been written without: Brooke Castillo, Tonya Leigh, Kendrick Shope, and Jenny Shih. Being a part of your inner circles has been one of the greatest gifts of my life. Entrepreneurship is lonely and it's easy to feel like everyone else has it figured out. Your vulnerability, transparency, and love will always be a part of my journey as an entrepreneur. Thanks for removing the veil and making it safe for me to do the same. I am grateful for your friendship.

Finally, to my boys Jesse and Lauti, my co-parent and friend-for-life Mila, and my generous and handsome husband, Paul. None of this would mean anything if I couldn't share it with you. Thank you for loving me with or without a phone glued to my hand.

difference press

Difference Press offers solopreneurs, including life coaches, healers, consultants, and community leaders, a comprehensive solution to get their books written, published, and promoted. A boutique-style alternative to self-publishing, Difference Press boasts a fair and easy-to-understand profit structure, low-priced author copies, and author-friendly contract terms. Its founder, Dr. Angela Lauria, has been bringing to life the literary ventures of hundreds of authors-in-transformation since 1994.

LET'S START A MOVEMENT WITH YOUR MESSAGE

You've seen other people make a difference with a book. Now it's your turn. If you are ready to stop watching and start taking massive action. Reach out.

"Yes, I'm ready!"

In a market where hundreds of thousands books are published every year and are never heard from again, all participants of The Author Incubator have bestsellers that are actively changing lives and making a difference.

In less than two years we've created over 100 bestselling books in a row, 90% from first-time authors. As a result, our regular book programs are selling out in advance and we are selecting only the highest quality and highest potential applicants for our future programs.

Our program doesn't just teach you how to write a book—our team of coaches, developmental editors, copy editors, art directors, and marketing experts incubate you from book idea to published bestseller, ensuring that the book you create can actually make a difference in the world. We only work with the people who will use their book to get out there and make that difference.

If you have life-or world-changing ideas or services, a servant's heart, and the willingness to do what it REALLY takes to make a difference in the world with your book, go to http://theAuthorIncubator.com/apply to complete an application for the program today.

*Better Videos:
Stand out. Be Seen.
Create Clients.*

by Rachel Dunn

*Embodied
Healing: Using
Yoga to Recover
from Trauma and
Extreme Stress*

by Lisa Danylchuk

*Evolve Your Life:
Rethink Your
Biggest Picture
Through Conscious
Evolution*

by Sheila Cash

*Growing Your
Separate Ways:
8 Straight Steps to
Separating with the
Same Intention of
Love and Respect
You Had...*

by Leah Ruppel

*How to Want Sex
Again: Rekindling
Passion with EFT*

by Alina Frank

*Invisible Dad:
How to Heal as a
Fatherless Daughter*

by Candice Ragland

*Not Your Average
5K: A Practical
8-Week Training
Plan for Beginning
Runners*

by Jill Angie

*The Cancer
Whisperer: How
to Let Cancer
Heal Your Life*

by Sophie Sabbage

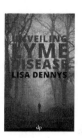

The Unfair Affair: How to Strengthen and Save Your Marriage, or Move on with Confidence, After Infidelity

by Wendy Kay

Untame Yourself: Reconnect to the Lost Art, Power and Freedom of Being a Woman

by Elizabeth DiAlto

Unveiling Lyme Disease: Is This What's Behind Your Chronic Illness?

by Lisa Dennys

Waking Up With Dogs: Beginning at the End

by Melissa Courtney

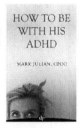

Whoops! I Forgot To Achieve My Potential: Create Your Very Own Personal Change Management Strategy to Get the...

by Maggie Huffman

Personal Finance That Doesn't Suck: A 5-step Guide to Quit Budgeting, Start Wealth Building and Get the Most from...

by Mindy Crary

Good Baby, Bad Sleeper: Discover Your Child's Sleep Personality To Finally Get the Sleep You Need

by Stephanie Hope Dodd

How You Can Be with His ADHD: What You Can Do To Rescue Your Relationship When Your Partner Has Adult ADHD

by Mark Julian

Made in United States
Orlando, FL
11 June 2022

18704802R00115